PENGUIN CLASSICS 🐧 DELUXE EDITION

LEAVES OF GRASS

WALT WHITMAN (1819–1892) was born on Long Island and educated in Brooklyn, New York. He served as a printer's devil, journeyman compositor, and itinerant schoolteacher, edited the *Long Islander*, and in 1846 became editor of *The Brooklyn Eagle*, a position from which he was discharged for political reasons. After a period in New Orleans, considered seminal in shaping his philosophy, he returned to Brooklyn. Although he had earlier affected the mien of a dandy, he now dressed as a "rough," and became prominent among the bohemian element of New York. In 1855 he published *Leaves of Grass*, which he continued to revise and republish over his lifetime. The Civil War found him working as an unofficial nurse to Northern and Southern soldiers in army hospitals in Washington, D.C. After the war he became a clerk in the Indian Bureau of the Department of the Interior, from which he was shortly dismissed by the Secretary on the grounds that *Leaves of Grass* was an immoral book. During his last nineteen years he lived in Camden, New Jersey. Although not previously neglected, he was particularly in the public eye during these years, when such English writers as William Michael Rossetti, A. C. Swinburne, J. A. Symonds, and Robert Louis Stevenson contended that Americans did not fully appreciate him. Among his works are *Drum-Taps* (1865), *Democratic Vistas* and *Passage to India* (1871), and *Specimen Days* (1882).

HAROLD BLOOM is Sterling Professor of Humanities at Yale University, where he has taught since 1955. His thirty books include *The Anxiety of Influence*, *The Book of J*, *The Western Canon*, *How to Read and Why*, *Shakespeare: The Invention of the Human*, *Where Shall Wisdom Be Found?*, *Genius*, and *The Names Divine: Jesus and Yahweh*. He has received the Gold Medal for Criticism from the American Academy of Arts and Letters, and the International Prize of Catalonia, the Alfonso Reyes Prize of Mexico, and the Hans Christian Andersen Bicentennial Prize of Denmark.

WALT WHITMAN'S
Leaves of Grass
THE FIRST (1855) EDITION

Introduction by HAROLD BLOOM

PENGUIN BOOKS

PENGUIN BOOKS

Published by the Penguin Group

Penguin Group (USA) Inc., 375 Hudson Street, New York, New York 10014, U.S.A.
Penguin Group (Canada), 90 Eglinton Avenue East, Suite 700, Toronto, Ontario,
Canada M4P 2Y3 (a division of Pearson Penguin Canada Inc.)
Penguin Books Ltd, 80 Strand, London WC2R 0RL, England
Penguin Ireland, 25 St Stephen's Green, Dublin 2, Ireland
(a division of Penguin Books Ltd)
Penguin Group (Australia), 250 Camberwell Road, Camberwell, Victoria 3124,
Australia (a division of Pearson Australia Group Pty Ltd)
Penguin Books India Pvt Ltd, 11 Community Centre, Panchsheel Park,
New Delhi – 110 017, India
Penguin Group (NZ), 67 Apollo Drive, Rosedale, North Shore 0632, New Zealand
(a division of Pearson New Zealand Ltd)
Penguin Books (South Africa) (Pty) Ltd, 24 Sturdee Avenue,
Rosebank, Johannesburg 2196, South Africa

Penguin Books Ltd, Registered Offices:
80 Strand, London WC2R 0RL, England

First published in the United States of America by Rome Brothers 1855
This edition with an introduction by Harold Bloom published in Penguin Books 2005

29th Printing

LIBRARY OF CONGRESS CATALOGING-IN-PUBLICATION DATA
Whitman, Walt, 1819–1892.
Leaves of grass : the first (1855) edition / Walt Whitman ; introduction by Harold Bloom.
p. cm. — (Penguin classics)
ISBN 978-0-14-303927-3
I. Title. II. Series.
PS3201 1855e
811'.3—dc22   2005047641

Printed in the United States of America
Set in Sabon

Contents

[1]The poems had no titles in the first edition. The titles listed here, for the convenience of readers, are the ones that Whitman finally chose for them.

Introduction and Celebration

You can nominate a fair number of literary works as candidates for the secular Scripture of the United States of America. They might include Herman Melville's *Moby-Dick*, Mark Twain's *Adventures of Huckleberry Finn*, Ralph Waldo Emerson's two series of *Essays* and *The Conduct of Life*, and arguably there are others. None of those, not even Emerson's, are as central as the first edition of *Leaves of Grass* (1855). Simmering until brought to a boil by Emerson (Whitman's own admission, later withdrawn), the American bard, our Homer and our Milton, broke the new road for the New World. D. H. Lawrence, alternately furious at Whitman and in thrall to him, saw his precursor as the poet of the Evening Land, sharing in Melville's litany for the doom of "the white race." The twentieth century's dominant American writer, William Faulkner, carried on from Melville in what now can be read as a tetralogy: *As I Lay Dying*, *The Sound and the Fury*, *Light in August*, and *Absalom, Absalom!* Cormac McCarthy's *Blood Meridian* is an epilogue to Melville and to Faulkner. Whitman's true heirs at home included T. S. Eliot's *The Waste Land*, Hart Crane's *The Bridge*, and Wallace Stevens's *The Auroras of Autumn*. Abroad, the catalog is too large for quick compilation: Lawrence, Lorca, Pessoa, Vallejo, Neruda, Borges, Paz are perhaps the most notable.

Walt Whitman was a Quaker, by family tradition, though this was the dissenting Quakerism of Elias Hicks, both Native American and African American, who had returned to the visionary

George Fox, founder of the once enthusiastic faith that Philadelphia had tamed. Hicks was a fiery preacher, and the boy Whitman never forgot his example, though the Gnostic Emerson and the Epicurean Fanny Wright combined to confirm the mature Whitman in his post-Christian stance. Walt Whitman in *Leaves of Grass* (1855) became the crucial celebrant of what I think we yet will call the American Religion, which commenced in the Cane Ridge Revival of 1800, where all denominations momentarily fused in an amalgam of Enthusiasm and Gnosticism, which marked the beginning of the end of European Protestantism in America. The Southern Baptists, Pentecostalists, Mormons, Adventists, and other native strains are ongoing emanations of what began at Cane Ridge. Our theologians and prophets of the American Religion include Emerson, Joseph Smith, and Horace Bushnell, among others. The philosopher William James is its psychologist, and Walt Whitman forever will be its poet-prophet, since he sings only songs of myself. We now have an American Jesus and an American Holy Spirit, and have largely banished Yahweh, except that he marches in as Warrior God, endlessly trampling out the vintage where the grapes of wrath are stored.

Many times every week I confront an ongoing flood of letters, manuscripts, proof-copies, and books calling upon me for response. Old and overworked, I ruefully recall the advice of Edmund Wilson, who kindly gave me his famous postcard: "Edmund Wilson does not," followed by a series of boxes to check where appropriate: "read unsolicited manuscripts and books, give lectures, recommend works to editors," and so forth. I gave Wilson back the card, murmuring that I surely would never require it, but the critical elder was an accurate prophet. I mention this because I am haunted by Emerson's magnificent response to receiving the first *Leaves of Grass* in the post:

Concord, Massachusetts, 21 *July, 1855*

DEAR SIR—I am not blind to the worth of the wonderful gift of "Leaves of Grass." I find it the most extraordinary piece of wit

& wisdom that America has yet contributed. I am very happy in reading it, as great power makes us happy. It meets the demand I am always making of what seemed the sterile & stingy nature, as if too much handiwork or too much lymph in the temperament were making our western wits fat & mean. I give you joy of your free & brave thought. I have great joy in it. I find incomparable things said incomparably well, as they must be. I find the courage of treatment, which so delights us, & which large perception only can inspire. I greet you at the beginning of a great career, which yet must have had a long foreground somewhere, for such a start. I rubbed my eyes a little to see if this sunbeam were no illusion; but the solid sense of the book is a sober certainty. It has the best merits, namely, of fortifying & encouraging.

I did not know until I, last night, saw the book advertised in a newspaper, that I could trust the name as real & available for a post-office. I wish to see my benefactor, & have felt much like striking my tasks, & visiting New York to pay you my respects.

R. W. Emerson

One century and a half later, it is still "the most extraordinary piece of wit & wisdom that America has yet contributed." What wit and wisdom Emerson showed in commending Whitman for wit and wisdom, rather than for exuberance and democracy, though both those seem evident enough. A lean and generous wit is discovered by Concord's Sage, who twice expresses joy for "thought" manifesting courage and freedom (for which Emerson's synonym is "wildness").

Treatment is the key, as indeed it is, and that mode relies upon a singularity of perception. Emerson was to age into some reservations, which from his perspective were legitimate. The Concord visionary was the American Plotinus to his own Plato; Whitman in 1855 already was more Epicurean than Platonist, and "Sun-Down Poem" ("Crossing Brooklyn Ferry") in the 1856 second *Leaves of Grass*, and "Elemental Drifts" ("As I Ebb'd with the Ocean of Life") in the third (1860), confirmed the Lucretianism in which Whitman stands midway between

Shelley and Wallace Stevens. Metaphysically, Whitman and
Emerson were opposed, though Emerson shrewdly found in
Whitman a student, like Thoreau, of "Self-Reliance." It was
not the Genteel Tradition that (partly) divided these two great
Americans: in some regards Emerson was more Redskin to
Whitman's Paleface. I would define the difference by invoking
Gershom Scholem, the Miltonic Jerusalem scholar of Kab-
balah, who loved Whitman and found in him a new Kabbalah:
"Walt Whitman revealed in an utterly naturalistic world what
kabbalists . . . revealed in their world" (*On Jews and Judaism
in Crisis*, 1976, p. 48).

Whitman restores the primal androgyne "Adam early in the
morning." The Anthropos of the Hermetic Corpus, the Adam
Kadmon of Kabbalah, revives in Walt Whitman, one of the
roughs, an American. We are accustomed to Whitman as Asian
(Hindu, Buddhist): he is our *Vedas*, our *Bhagavad-Gita*, our *Su-
tras*. But he is also our *Zohar*, an esotericist of extraordinary
originality. In Kabbalah, Enoch, without dying, becomes the
angel Metatron or lesser Yahweh. In Christian Kabbalah,
Enoch is the anointed one, Christ. Emerson was Elijah or John
the Baptist to Whitman's American Christ. Is not Walt as enig-
matic, elusive, evasive, fascinating as the Jesus of Mark's
Gospel? Emerson invented the American Religion; Whitman
incarnated it. In an astonishing passage, Wallace Stevens cele-
brated Whitman as both the American Moses and the American
Aaron:

> In the far South the sun of autumn is passing
> Like Walt Whitman walking along a ruddy shore.
> He is singing and chanting the things that are part of him,
> The worlds that were and will be, death and day.
> Nothing is final, he chants. No man shall see the end.
> His beard is of fire and his staff is a leaping flame.

It is another irony that no other poet, not Lorca or Hart Crane
or Pessoa, has celebrated Whitman so definitively as the genteel
Stevens, who professed to be offended by Walt's Tramp per-
sona, loafing and inviting the soul. Stevens is never straight

about Whitman, but neither were T. S. Eliot and Ezra Pound. The poet James Wright accurately spoke of "the old man Walt Whitman," and the few major American poets of the twentieth century not begotten by Whitman include Robert Frost, Marianne Moore, Robert Penn Warren, Elizabeth Bishop, and James Merrill. Most of the others—Stevens, Hart Crane, Eliot, Aiken, Pound, W. C. Williams, Jeffers, John Wheelwright, Roethke, Ammons, Ashbery, Merwin, James Wright—have a complex relation to *Leaves of Grass*. The major women poets owe much to Emily Dickinson—Moore, Bishop, May Swenson, Amy Clampitt, the Canadian Anne Carson—as does the African American Robert Hayden, while the other major black poet, Jay Wright, is profoundly Whitmanian.

In proportion to his actual aesthetic achievement, Whitman remains undervalued and misunderstood. He is the greatest artist his nation has brought forth, but such judgment needs to be taken further. No comparable figure in the arts has emerged from the last four centuries in the Americas: North, Central, South, or the Caribbean. Whitman's peers are Milton, Bach, Michelangelo, baroque masters of sublimity. *Paradise Lost*, the endless fecundity of Bach, the continuous glory of the Sistine ceiling are equaled by the sequence of Whitman's six major poems: "Song of Myself," "The Sleepers," "Crossing Brooklyn Ferry," and the triad of elegies: "Out of the Cradle Endlessly Rocking," "As I Ebb'd with the Ocean of Life," and "When Lilacs Last in the Dooryard Bloom'd." To call Walt Whitman at his strongest baroque must seem initially paradoxical in regard to a poet who professes to chant "Spontaneous Me," but Whitman is no improviser. His artistry reflects conscious study of his precursors in the language despite his American nationalist ambivalence toward British tradition. He professed to find William Cullen Bryant equal to William Wordsworth, and said that Shelley the man meant more to him than Shelley's poetry. Discounting any statements by strong poets on their precursors is good policy: "The Sleepers" has a complex relation to Shelley's visionary "The Witch of Atlas," and "As I Ebb'd with the Ocean of Life" reverberates with tonalities of "Ode to the West Wind." Keats's Negative Capability roused Whitman to a defense of his own "powerful press of himself . . . his own masterly identity."

Tennyson, his exact contemporary, troubled Whitman rather the way that William Butler Yeats challenged Wallace Stevens, or T. S. Eliot provoked Hart Crane. In October 1855, a few months after the appearance of the first *Leaves of Grass*, Whitman condemned Tennyson for "supercilious elegance," but this defensive remark counts for little when you catch the echoes of Tennyson in the "Lilacs" elegy, which covertly is written agonistically to overgo the laureate of "Maud," "In Memoriam," and the Wellington "Ode."

Whitman, wary of Shakespeare, weakly characterized the poet of *King Lear* as "feudalistic," but this warding-off gesture is set aside by the extraordinary moment in "Crossing Brooklyn Ferry" when the American bard identifies himself with Lear's godson Edgar, in an allusion too overt to be evaded. The more deeply you read Whitman, the more you encounter his suppressed allusiveness, his gathering self-awareness of the complexities of poetic tradition that he urges himself to usurp. In his battle for self-reliance, he remains Shakespearean and High Romantic, as much a Wordsworthian as Emerson himself. Unlike Emerson, he had the prophet of "Self-Reliance" as his literary father, and to that enormous (and resented) indebtedness I turn.

2

Franz Kafka cryptically remarked that he would have composed "a new Kabbalah," except for the Zionist revival. Walter Benjamin and Gershom Scholem, who always maintained their close friendship, despite Scholem's transition to Jerusalem and Benjamin's suicidal refusal to depart from Europe, understood best what Kafka might have meant by "the Kabbalah of Franz Kafka."

When I first met Scholem and his wife, Fania, in Jerusalem, he dryly named me "his most suprising disciple." In several conversations then, and later in the United States, I listened intently as Scholem adumbrated his impressions of Walt Whitman, who seemed to the great sage of Kabbalistic scholarship a poet-prophet closer to the spirit of Kabbalah than was William Blake, who actually figures in the history of Christian Kabbalah. I had noted a number of places in Scholem's essays and interviews where he spoke of Whitman's sense of "the absolute holiness of absolute secularity" and found in Whitman the prophet of a naturalist Kabbalah.

Whitman vindicates Scholem's genius for detecting affinities. In "Song of Myself" we can regard Walt Whitman, one of the roughs, an American, as a return of the Kabbalistic Divine Man, the Adam Kadmon, and even of the undying Enoch transformed into the Angel Metatron, Prince of the Divine Countenance, or the lesser Yahweh. Another clear analogue is Walt as the Hermetic Anthropos, unfallen androgyne who beholds his image in the waters of night, and so plunges into the cosmos of love and death, the mother and the sea.

Scholars trace some of Whitman's origins to Eastern thought, or to Egyptian antiquities. These perhaps helped shape his curious analogues to Lurianic or "regressive" Kabbalah. Like the "without end" Yahweh of Luria, Whitman cannot concentrate himself without a withdrawal and contraction that he metaphorically masks as synecdochical one-in-many identifications, hyperbolical conflations with the rising sun, and amazing transmutations of his belatedness into what Wallace Stevens (involuntarily following Whitman) termed an "ever-early candor."

There are even similarities between Whitman's highly original psychic cartography—my self, my soul, and the real me or me myself—and the tripartite division of *nephesh*, *ru'ach*, and *neshamah* (called *naran* in Kabbalah). Jewish Neoplatonists from at least Abraham ibn Ezra onward first popularized these, but the early Kabbalists of Gerona transmuted them into stranger forms. *Neshamah* continued as the rational (more-or-less) soul, a Divine spark, while the *nephesh* was the vital principle or self, and the *ru'ach* remained the gift of breath with which Yahweh had first animated Adam. In Whitman, "my soul" is *nephesh*, "my self" is *ru'ach*, and "the real me" or "me myself" is *neshamah*. Whitman would not have known what to make of these comparisons, but they suggest aspects of his cartography at least as well as other traditions do.

What drove Whitman to *his* triad of psychic agencies? I suspect that his cartographic impulse arose as an apotropaic gesture, a warding-off directed against his indubitable catalyst, Emerson. Without Emerson on the American soul, Whitman would have gone on simmering perpetually, and *Leaves of Grass* could not have been composed. "An American Bard at last!" Whitman proclaimed in one of his self-reviews, yet if he was "Adam early in the morning," there remained the inconvenience of that endless experimenter with no past at his back, the Sage of Concord.

The dialectic of Myself and the Real Me or Me Myself was personal and not particularly Emersonian, but the greater mystery for Whitman was the unknowable soul. Rough Walt was something of a reaction-formation against Walter Whitman Sr., archetypal carpenter-father, Joseph to his son's Jesus, while the daemonic Real Me was precisely that, reality. The fiercely sullen mother, endlessly crying for her castaways, is already merging with night, death, and the sea in "The Sleepers," the astonishing "I wander all night in my vision" in the 1855 *Leaves of Grass*.

The poet James Wright celebrated "the old man, Walt Whitman" for his "delicacy" of poetic form. The nuances of soul are part of that delicacy also. Mutlu Blasing, an authority on American poetry's rhetoric of forms, rightly notes how Whitman's identification of consciousness with night, death, the mother, and the sea develops first in "The Sleepers," 1855 version. Chapter 4 of Emerson's manifesto, *Nature* (1836), seems to be Whitman's hidden source on the problem of his soul, together with a gnomic passage from *The Over-Soul* (1838):

> The soul looketh steadily forwards, creating a world before her, leaving worlds behind her. She has no dates, nor rites, nor persons, nor speculations, nor men. *The soul knows only the soul . . .*

If the soul knows only the soul, what can make it knowable by what in us is not-soul? Emerson calls such knowability "power," and praised this "power" as the great contribution of *Leaves of Grass* (1855). The synonyms for power in Emerson are "will" and "vitality," which are opposed to "the sterile & stingy nature." Vitality wishes to express itself, for Whitman, through the love of comrades, but generally had to be content with autoeroticism, the characteristic sexuality of "Song of Myself." I recall wandering about New York City thirty years back with Kenneth Burke, my prime catalyst in the transition between two books, *The Anxiety of Influence* (1973) and *A Map of Misreading* (1975). Burke had a particular regard for Whitman's poem "Spontaneous Me" (originally called "Bunch Poem"), and gleefully compared Whitman's masturbatory Muse to Goethe's conclusions of each of the five acts of the Second Part of *Faust*. When I observed to my genial mentor that the boundaries between literal and figurative in Whitman wavered incessantly, he gleefully assented, which led me to wonder how metaphoric the homoeroticism of Whitman's poetry (even of his life) might prove to have been. If all is trope except in games, then Whitman indeed was in and out of the game and watching and wondering at it.

But Whitman's prime trope is not the vital Myself or the homoerotic double of the Real Me / Me Myself, but the fourfold Soul, the haunting litany: Night, Death, the Mother, the Sea. Though it is a universal and immemorial metaphor, Walt Whitman rendered a peculiarly American version of this ancient figuration. He wanted to reassert the power of his poetic mind over the universe of death. As American Jesus, he longed for the day, resurrection, the father, the shoreline, and of this longing he created *the* poem of our climate, what James Wright named the Shore-Ode, the American transformation of Wordsworth's English Romantic Crisis-Ode. Our answers to Wordsworth's "Intimations of Immortality . . . ," Coleridge's "Dejection: an Ode," Shelley's "Ode to the West Wind," and Keats's Great Odes are "The Sleepers" and Whitman's subsequent elegies for the self: "Out of the Cradle Endlessly Rocking," "As I Ebb'd with the Ocean of Life," and "When Lilacs Last in the Dooryard Bloom'd."

The implicit burden of the Wordsworthian crisis-ode is:

experiential loss is compensated by imaginative gain. Emerson's iron law of Compensation states: "Nothing is got for nothing," an American version of Lear's warning to Cordelia: "Nothing will come of nothing—Speak again." The Whitmanian shore-ode is therefore darker than the British High Romantic greater lyric, inevitable since Wordsworth and Shelley were not messiahs as was Walt Whitman.

3

If "Walt Whitman" were a Shakespearean character, then we might know better how to respond to Emerson's wonderment as to the "long foreground" of the 1855 *Leaves of Grass*. Scholars and biographers keep charting that foreground, but have not worked through the difficulties of Whitman's marvelous metamorphosis in the winter of 1854–55. Nearing the middle of the journey, Walter Whitman Jr. went home again, and by springtime emerged as Walt Whitman, still the greatest writer engendered by the New World, whether in American English, Spanish, Portuguese, or French. None of the possible rivals in the United States is finally of Whitman's eminence: not Emily Dickinson, Emerson, Herman Melville, Nathaniel Hawthorne, Mark Twain, Henry James, or William Faulkner. Only Dickinson approaches Whitman among the poets; even the strongest of the twentieth century trail behind the Whitmanian Sublime: Robert Frost, Wallace Stevens, T. S. Eliot, Marianne Moore, Hart Crane, Elizabeth Bishop, James Merrill, A. R. Ammons, John Ashbery. Walt stops somewhere waiting for them.

After the decade 1840–1850, Whitman ceased to be a *flaneur* and journalist in Manhattan, and went back to his family. He built houses with his father and brothers, and he wrote, sometimes for several hours a day. His reading was hungry and intense, perhaps most passionate when he immersed himself in the essays of Emerson.

I hear Emerson most intensively in the early notebook fragments that were to be fused into "Song of Myself" (untitled in 1855, like every other poem in the first *Leaves of Grass*). Here is the earliest fragment in which we encounter what will be the central poem of the New World:

> I am your voice—It was tied in you—In me it begins to talk.
> I celebrate myself to celebrate every man and woman alive;
> I loosen the tongue that was tied in them,
> It begins to talk out of my mouth.
>
> I celebrate myself to celebrate you:
> I say the same word for every man and woman alive.
> And I say that the soul is not greater than the body,
> And I say that the body is not greater than the soul.

The "I" and the "you" in Whitman are neither separate nor unified. John Ashbery is closer to Whitman in this paradox than the other descendants of *Leaves of Grass*, though there are parallels in Fernando Pessoa, T. S. Eliot, Wallace Stevens, and D. H. Lawrence. Yet none of these, even Ashbery, generously affirm that: "I celebrate myself to celebrate you." I have titled this introduction a "celebration," not only because it is now a century and a half since *Leaves of Grass* first was published, but also to show gratitude to Whitman. Who except Whitman could have so greatly redeemed the entire tradition of Western literature? I can think of no other poet who addresses the reader as directly:

> Closer yet I approach you,
> What thought you have of me now, I had as much of you—
>   I laid in my stores in advance,
> I consider'd long and seriously of you before you were born.
>
> Who was to know what should come home to me?
> Who knows but I am enjoying this?
> Who knows, for all the distance, but I am as good as looking at
>   you now, for all you cannot see me?

What made this possible? How could the "Sun-Down Poem" of the second *Leaves of Grass* (1856), later retitled "Crossing

Brooklyn Ferry," change so radically the immemorial covenant of intimate separations between reader and poet? Shakespeare's preternatural power is the creation of personalities capable of *self-overhearing*. Whitman's urgent power is *immediacy*. Of Whitmanian inwardness we know little, because he is endlessly evasive, and mystifies himself. The inwardness of Shakespeare is a willed blank, the center of a target we never hit. Stagecraft alone, like Tudor-Stuart history, cannot account for the uniqueness of Falstaff and Hamlet, Iago and Cleopatra, or the shattering of Lear's and Macbeth's worlds. Cultural politics of the United States from 1830 to 1870 does not divulge the secret of Whitman's breakthrough into the confident ecstasy of the outsetting bard:

> I celebrate myself to celebrate you:
> I say the same word for every man and woman alive.
> And I say that the soul is not greater than the body,
> And I say that the body is not greater than the soul.

"Mysticism" is a hopeless word for Whitmanian reality. If I invoke Kabbalah (following Scholem's hints), I repeat my admonitions from elsewhere that "Jewish mysticism" is a misleading term for Kabbalah, though it has been sanctified by Scholem and by Moshe Idel. The American Religion, despite its maskings, is not mystical. Primary to our natural faith, which I argue began in 1800 with the Cane Ridge Revivals on the Kentucky-Tennessee border, are three barely repressed convictions: the God within, the freedom of solitude shared only with that God, and the conviction that one's best and most ancient residue never was part of nature or creation. Whitman, in that fecund winter of 1854–55, came to know that he was what Kabbalah named Adam Kadmon, or what William Blake had called Albion, the Ancient Man, as in this early Whitmanian fragment:

> Of God I know not;
> But this I know;
> I can comprehend no being more wonderful than man;

Man, before the rage of whose passions the storms of Heaven
   are but a breath;
Before whose caprices the lightning is slow and less fatal;
Man, microcosm of all Creation's wildness, terror, beauty and
   power,
And whose folly and wickedness are in nothing else existent.
O dirt, you corpse, I reckon you are good manure—but that I
   do not smell—
I smell your beautiful white roses—
I kiss your leafy lips—I slide my hands for the brown melons of
   your breasts.

Doubtless, Whitman's deepest desires were homoerotic, but if
ever he acted fully on them, even in what seems to have been a
debacle in the winter of 1859–60, he evidently learned again
the pragmatic truth of his profound Onanism:

I merely stir, press, feel with my fingers, and am happy,
To touch my person to some one else's is about as much as I can
   stand.
                         —"Song of Myself," section 27

"Homosexual Poetics," yet another diversion of current aca-
demic cant, illuminates little in Whitman, who proudly speaks
for Onan. As a god, Walt resembles an Egyptian deity masturbat-
ing a cosmos into existence. Again, the early notebook fragments
that will exfoliate into "Song of Myself" are the point of origin:

One touch of a tug of me has unhaltered all my senses but feeling
That pleases the rest so, they have given up to it in submission
They are all emulous to swap themselves off for what it can do
   to them.
Every one must be a touch
Or else she will abdicate and nibble only at the edges of feeling.
They move caressingly up and down my body
They leave themselves and come with bribes to whatever part of
   me touches.—

To my lips, to the palms of my hands, and whatever my hands
    hold.
Each brings the best she had,
For each is in love with touch.
I do not wonder that one feeling now does so much for me,
He is free of all the rest,—and swiftly begets offspring of them,
    better than the dams.
A touch now reads me a library of knowledge in an instant.
It smells for me the fragrance of wine and lemon-blows.
It tastes for me with a tongue of its own,
It finds an ear wherever it rests or taps.
It brings the rest around it, and they all stand on a headland and
    mock me
They have left me to touch, and taken their place on a headland.
The sentries have deserted every other part of me
They have left me helpless to the torrent of touch
They have all come to the headland to witness and assist against
    me.—
I roam about drunk and stagger
I am given up by traitors,
I talk wildly I am surely out of my head,
I am myself the greatest traitor.
I went myself first to the headland
Unloose me, touch, you are taking the breath from my throat!
Unbar your gates you are too much for me
Fierce Wrestler! do you keep your heaviest grip for the last?
Will you sting me most even at parting?
Will you struggle even at the threshold with spasms more
    delicious than all before?
Does it make you to ache so to leave me?
Do you wish to show me that even what you did before was
    nothing to what you can do?
Or have you and all the rest combined to see how much I can
    endure?
Pass as you will; take drops of my life, if that is what you are
    after
Only pass to some one else, for I can contain you no longer
I held more than I thought

> I did not think I was big enough for so much ecstasy
> Or that a touch could take it all out of me.

"I went myself first to the headland" is Whitman's crucial beginning as the New World's bard, however uncomfortable this may render some among us, many of my students included. Rarely discussed, this is Whitman's authentic scandal, his transgression of Taboo (aside from his incestuous union with the mother in the hermit-thrush's song of Death in the magnificent "Lilacs" elegy). Revising his central metaphor of "the headland" in "Song of Myself" 28, Whitman augmented his explicitness:

> I went myself first to the headland . . . . my own hands carried
> me there.

This headland is the psychic promontory that scrambling out onto produces the condition which Ludwig Binswanger called *Verstiegenheit*, wittily translated by Jacob Needleman as Extravagance, relying upon *extra vagans* as "beyond all limits." You scramble onto the headland in so many ways (of which Onanism is a mere figuration) and find you cannot make your way back unaided. Sigmund Freud, who mentored Binswanger (though not in the fusion of psychoanalysis and Heidegger), understood this psychic extravagance as a secular variant of Yahwistic Exodus. Abram (who becomes Abraham) and Moses are ordered to perform *yetziat*, a "getting out" into the Wilderness, away from all bondage, whether in Chaldean Ur or Egypt, the land of death. This movement of the Real Me or Me Myself is Whitman's also, part of his Hicksite Quaker heritage. Agata Bielek-Robson sees this, in the Hebrews, as a call to singularity, which cares, rather than to individuality, which can be indifferent. Whitman's Exodus is *Leaves of Grass* (1855), in which his *hubris*, which ancient Gnostics named *pneuma*, "breath" or "spark," discovered itself in the Real Me or Me Myself. The house of bondage, both metrical and taboo-ridden, is abandoned by Whitman's defiance.

Like Elijah and John the Baptist, the bard of *Leaves of Grass* "gets out" into the Wilderness, yet that is a way station only, as

Whitman breaks his new road into the Canaan of a new American poetry, and yet that poetry is anything but formless: its paradigm is the King James Bible, and the nuances of Whitman's subtle prosody are derived by him ultimately from William Tyndale and Miles Coverdale, heroic geniuses of translation who form a stylistic sublimity equaled in English only by Chaucer, Shakespeare, Milton, Blake, Wordsworth, and Walt Whitman, the New World's own prophet of "getting out," as all his greatest disciples have seen: Pessoa, D. H. Lawrence, Lorca, Vallejo, Paz, Borges, Neruda, Stevens, Hart Crane, Ammons, Ashbery, and so many more. You need not affirm Whitman to be fathered by him: Ezra Pound (hardly tolerable, by me), T. S. Eliot, and Wallace Stevens rarely resemble Whitman on the surface, but he is the giant form swimming in their depths, and he will abide as the drowned man of "The Sleepers," its "beautiful gigantic swimmer."

4

Like Abraham and Moses, and Jesus in the Gospel of Thomas, Whitman is always "passing" by, getting out of bondage into the Wilderness, and then breaking from the Wasteland onto the Shores of America, led there by his prophet, Ralph Waldo Emerson. The early notebook fragments again are the seedbed of this getting-out, which is also a Resurrection:

> In vain were nails driven through my hands.
> I remember my crucifixion and bloody coronation
> I remember the mockers and the buffeting insults
> The sepulcher and the white linen have yielded me up
> I am alive in New York and San Francisco,
> Again I tread the streets after two thousand years.
> Not all the traditions can put vitality in churches
> They are not alive, they are cold mortar and brick,
> I can easily build as good, and so can you:—
> Books are not men—

There is no single pattern to these notebook fragments of 1854–55, yet they share in an exuberance of renewal, as though Whitman were returning to power now latent but once highly active. Only a week or two after writing Whitman his celebratory letter, Emerson mused in his journal that "it is the office of poets to suggest a vast wealth, a background, a divinity, out of which all this . . . springs." Can we isolate the precise Emersonian texts from which Whitman sprang in 1854–55? I tend to brood on *The Over-Soul* as one among them, not one of my own favorites, if only because I am not persuaded I understand it: "The soul knows only the soul."

Whitman would have endorsed the view just before that enigma:

> The soul looketh steadily forwards, creating a world before her, leaving worlds behind her.

In *Spiritual Laws*, which also means little to me, I suspect Whitman acquired a certain aspect of his own drive from a strong paragraph:

> A man's genius, the quality that differences him from every other, the susceptibility to one class of influences, the selection of what is fit for him, the rejection of what is unfit, determines for him the character of the universe. A man is a method, a progressive arrangement; a selecting principle, gathering his like to him, wherever he goes. He takes only his own out of the multiplicity that sweeps and circles round him. He is like one of those booms which are set out from the shore on rivers to catch driftwood, or like the loadstone amongst splinters of steel. Those facts, words, persons, which dwell in his memory without his being able to say why, remain, because they have a relation to him not less real for being as yet unapprehended. They are symbols of value to him, as they can interpret parts of his consciousness which he would vainly seek words for in the conventional images of books and other minds. What attracts my attention shall have it, as I will go to the man who knocks at my door, whilst a thousand persons, as

worthy, go by it, to whom I give no regard. It is enough that these particulars speak to me. A few anecdotes, a few traits of character, manners, face, a few incidents, have an emphasis in your memory out of all proportion to their apparent significance, if you measure them by the ordinary standards. They relate to your gift. Let them have their weight, and do not reject them, and cast about for illustration and facts more usual in literature. What your heart thinks great is great. The soul's emphasis is always right.

There is general agreement that for Whitman the central Emersonian text was *The Poet*, which leads off the second series of *Essays*. Few bring Whitman and Emerson together without emphasizing this paragraph in particular:

I look in vain for the poet whom I describe. We do not, with sufficient plainness, or sufficient profoundness, address ourselves to life, nor dare we chaunt our own times, and social circumstance. If we filled the day with bravery, we should not shrink from celebrating it. Time and nature yield us many gifts, but not yet the timely man, the new religion, the reconciler, whom all things await. Dante's praise is, that he dared to write his autobiography in colossal cipher, or into universality. We have yet had no genius in America, with tyrannous eye, which knew the value of our incomparable materials, and saw, in the barbarism and materialism of the times, another carnival of the same gods whose picture he so much admires in Homer; then in the middle age; then in Calvinism. Banks and tariffs, the newspaper and caucus, methodism and unitarianism, are flat and dull to dull people, but rest on the same foundations of wonder as the town of Troy, and the temple of Delphos, and are as swiftly passing away. Our logrolling, our stumps and their politics, our fisheries, the wrath of rogues, and the pusillanimity of honest men, the northern trade, the southern planting, the western clearing, Oregon, and Texas, are yet unsung. Yet America is a poem in our eyes; its ample geography dazzles the imagination, and it will not wait long for metres. If I have not found that excellent combination of gifts

in my countrymen which I seek, neither could I aid myself to fix
the idea of the poet by reading now and then in Chalmers's col-
lection of five centuries of English poets. These are wits, more
than poets, though there have been poets among them. But when
we adhere to the ideal of the poet, we have our difficulties even
with Milton and Homer. Milton is too literary, and Homer too
literal and historical.

These are, if any, the sentences that brought Whitman to his
boil, and they echo throughout the first *Leaves of Grass*. In the
volume's Preface, Emerson's aggressivity expands to Whitman's
pugnacity:

> There will soon be no more priests. Their work is done. They
> may wait awhile . . perhaps a generation or two . . dropping off
> by degrees. A superior breed shall take their place . . . . the
> gangs of kosmos and prophets en masse shall take their place. A
> new order shall arise and they shall be the priests of man, and
> every man shall be his own priest. The churches built under
> their umbrage shall be the churches of men and women.
> Through the divinity of themselves shall the kosmos and the
> new breed of poets be interpreters of men and women and of all
> events and things. They shall find their inspiration in real ob-
> jects today, symptoms of the past and future . . . . They shall not
> deign to defend immortality or God or the perfection of things
> or liberty or the exquisite beauty and reality of the soul. They
> shall arise in America and be responded to from the remainder
> of the earth.

This prophecy remains unfulfilled and unfulfillable, except in
certain groupings of American Religionists. Setting that aside, I
want now to work my way through *Leaves of Grass* (1855) as
Emerson first perused it. Twelve poems, untitled and oddly
punctuated with rows of four dots, appear in no rational se-
quence, starting with the masterwork not to be called "Song of
Myself" until 1881.

5

Kenneth Burke, writing a century after *Leaves of Grass* (1855), meditated upon the metaphoric "Leaves" and "Grass" of the grand title, while carefully avoiding any conclusive interpretation. John Hollander has pointed to the ambiguity of *Leaves "of" Grass*: what is that "of"?

What Wallace Stevens called "the fiction of the leaves" begins with Homer, and most notably passes to Vergil, Dante, Spenser, Milton, and Shelley before it undergoes Whitman's merger of the image of individual, Autumnal death with the Biblical metaphor of "all flesh is grass." Healthy grass survives winter, and yet hardly is an emblem of immortality. The dead leaves begin to prefigure a resurrection only in Shelley's "Ode to the West Wind," which Whitman echoes in "As I Ebb'd with the Ocean of Life." Yet *Grass of Leaves* hardly could be Whitman's title.

A printer by education, Whitman could have intended the title as an insouciant throwaway: leaves are printers' sheets, and grass, extempore stuff thrown in to fill them up. Whitmanian comedy always is blended with the spirit's splendor, and leaves of grass suggests a cure for the fiction of the leaves. In the overtly homoerotic longings of *Calamus* ("sweet flag," or the Whitmanian phallic emblem), there is a lovely three-line poem cited by Burke:

> Here the frailest leaves of me and yet my strongest lasting,
> Here I shade and hide my thoughts, I myself do not expose
>   them,
> And yet they expose me more than all my other poems.

Are these leaves only pages in Whitman's book? They are that, and something more intimately housed in him. Perhaps they would not have emerged fully except for the central phase of the poet's life, his beautiful daily unpaid service in the war hospitals of Washington, D.C., from 1861 to 1865, between the ages of forty-two through forty-six. Wound-dresser, nurse, comforter, bringer of little gifts (clean underwear, letter-writing paper, fruit, brandy, and some hope), Whitman spent what money he could earn and cadge, and spent more of his self than he had known he possessed. Something vital in his poetry began to burn out: its last stand is in the "Lilacs" elegy, to me his greatest poem (a judgment he prophetically rejected), as it was to William and Henry James.

The wounded soldiers, the dying in particular, became Whitman's leaves; their mutilated flesh what he had seen as grass. A decade after he wrote it, Whitman vindicated the only American metaphor that deserves to be called Homeric:

> And now it seems to me the beautiful uncut hair of graves.

6

D. H. Lawrence told us that the Americans are unworthy of their Whitman. How could we not be, whether in 1855 or 2005? Yet absorbing him is a process that has taken me a lifetime, and is not over yet. I have murmured his longer poems out loud to myself, while recovering from major surgery, in hospital and at home. There is, I think, little sentimentality in my conviction that reciting him, and brooding alike upon his celebrations and his elegies, helped heal me, hastening a little the terribly slow pace of recovering from trauma. Walt Whitman remains, for secularists, our national healer, as much the poet of the American Religion as American Jesus and the Holy Spirit are its gods. It is scarcely blasphemy to aver that Whitman has joined that pantheon. Like his master Emerson, he thought prayer a disease of the will, and so I do not pray to him, but I seek his Blessing, for he had the gift of bestowing more life, as thousands of ill and wounded soldiers, Union and Confederate, white and black, discovered. Whitman could not bless us except through aesthetic splendor. He thought capaciously, but without the original cognitive power of Emerson and of Emily Dickinson, and unlike Emerson and William James he was not primarily a wisdom writer. But what James Wright termed Whitman's "delicacy" of form and diction is unmatched by any other American poet, not even Dickinson, Frost, Stevens, Eliot, Hart Crane, Elizabeth Bishop.

Superb as the aesthetic eminence reached in the 1855 *Leaves of Grass* remains, I increasingly agree with Roy Harvey Pearce that the finest single volume of Whitman is the third edition, *Leaves of Grass* (1860), though it necessarily lacks "When Lilacs Last in the Dooryard Bloom'd," Whitman's sunset glory. We still need a Variorum Whitman, a giant volume that would print, in sequence, the five editions that matter most: 1855, 1856, 1860, *Drum-Taps* and *Sequel*, 1865, and the 1891 "deathbed" volume, approved by the poet a year before his departure. Such a book should begin with the notebook fragments of 1854–55. Perhaps the bicentenary of *Leaves of Grass* in 2055 will bring forth that great book, the treasure of our nation.

7

What were later to be named as "Song of Myself," "The Sleepers," "There Was a Child Went Forth," and "Who Learns My Lesson Complete?" are the four indispensable poems of the 1855 *Leaves of Grass*. Though Hicksite Quakerism gave Whitman his beautiful reliance upon the stylistics of the authorized version of the English Bible, and his rhetorical strategy of testimony as if in a spiritual meeting, critics too often relate *Leaves of Grass* to one Martin Tupper rather than to William Wordsworth's autobiographical mode. Emerson, a prose Wordsworthian (and Coleridgeian), is mostly casual in his self-references, yet these also sanctioned Whitman's only apparent disclosures. Unlike Emerson, Whitman never read Wordsworth's 1850 *Prelude*, but he had pondered "Ode: Intimations of Immortality from Recollections of Earliest Childhood." My long impression is that Whitman, in his formative time, read intensively rather than widely. "Crossing Brooklyn Ferry" vitally echoes the recalcitrantly heroic Edgar of *King Lear*, and phantasmagoria in "The Sleepers" knowingly touches the wilder edges of

Tennyson, once amiably acknowledged by Whitman as "the boss-man of us all."

There is a public misperception that finds Ginsberg and Kerouac rather than Stevens and Eliot as Whitman's authentic continuators. Every dominant image cluster in *The Waste Land* is quarried from the "Lilacs" lament for Lincoln, and Eliot nears conclusion of his exodus into the wilderness with the eloquent: "These fragments I have shored against my ruins," which alludes unmistakably to "As I Ebb'd with the Ocean of Life." Ginsberg charmingly sees Walt Whitman at the supermarket, but can that survive when juxtaposed with Wallace Stevens's epiphany of Whitman as the American Sublime?

In prose, Stevens ruefully kept deprecating Whitman's Tramp persona, fearing that the American public might therefore judge the Hartford seer as Man on the Dump. How extraordinary then was his dazzling and tremendous vision of Walt Whitman as the American Moses and Aaron fused into one antiapocalyptic messiah of our literary culture. Hart Crane, audaciously declaring Walt his true father as opposed to Clarence Crane, inventor of the candy LifeSaver, hymned Whitman in *The Bridge* as the Angel of America, prophetic of later angelic descents in Tennessee Williams and Tony Kushner. Williams, when I met him, proudly showed me his constant companion, Crane's *Collected Poems*, pilfered from the Washington University of St. Louis library. Kushner slyly appropriates Whitman wherever he can, and owes considerably more to our national poet than to the egregious Bert Brecht, endless plagiarizer of three women of genius carried about in his portable harem.

Inescapable all but everywhere, Whitman finally captured even the aging Henry James, who in his youth had reviewed *Drum-Taps* as the effort of an essentially prosaic mind to lift itself by muscular exertion into poetry. The American public, the brash young Henry insisted, would reject Whitman in the name of their higher culture. Much wiser, the master of the American novel would ask that "Lilacs" be read aloud to him, and wept (as I do) at the magnificence of our greatest poem's closing harmonies:

Yet each to keep and all, retrievements out of the night,
The song, the wondrous chant of the gray-brown bird,
And the tallying chant, the echo arous'd in my soul,
With the lustrous and drooping star with the countenance full of
    woe,
With the holders holding my hand nearing the call of the bird,
Comrades mine and I in the midst, and their memory ever I
    keep, for the dead I loved so well,
For the sweetest, wisest soul of all my days and lands—and this
    for his dear sake,
Lilac and star and bird twined with the chant of my soul,
There in the fragrant pines and the cedars dusk and dim.

That is a decade later than the first *Leaves of Grass*, but its more-
than-Tennysonian organ tonalities are the antithetical comple-
tions of the confident simplicity that opens itself to us in 1855:

I celebrate myself,
And what I assume, you shall assume,
For every atom belonging to me as good belongs to you.

I loafe and invite my soul,
I lean and loafe at my ease . . . . observing a spear of summer
    grass.

How does one *invite* one's soul? Who, what is being invited, and
to what revel? Whitman knows his rough self as an enabling fic-
tion, and his real self as his Fancy or Muse. Of his soul he knows
virtually nothing yet senses already that it dwells out in the moth-
ering night and the sea's universe of death. The Quaker carpenter
father was a self rougher than his son's fictive self, but of Louisa
the mother we are told only that her deepest erotic attachment
came in her youth well before her marriage to Whitman's father:

Now I tell what my mother told me today as we sat at dinner
    together,
Of when she was a nearly grown girl living home with her
    parents on the old homestead.

A red squaw came one breakfasttime to the old homestead,
On her back she carried a bundle of rushes for rushbottoming
     chairs;
Her hair straight shiny coarse black and profuse halfenveloped
     her face,
Her step was free and elastic . . . . her voice sounded exquisitely
     as she spoke.

My mother looked in delight and amazement at the stranger,
She looked at the beauty of her tallborne face and full and
     pliant limbs,
The more she looked upon her she loved her,
Never before had she seen such wonderful beauty and purity;
She made her sit on a bench by the jamb of the fireplace . . . .
     she cooked food for her,
She had no work to give her but she gave her remembrance and
     fondness.

The red squaw staid all the forenoon, and toward the middle of
     the afternoon she went away;
O my mother was loth to have her go away,
All the week she thought of her . . . . she watched for her many
     a month,
She remembered her many a winter and many a summer,
But the red squaw never came nor was heard of there again.

Whitman, more subtly sophisticated than most of us, senses
that his homoeroticism is allied to his mother's unfulfilled long-
ing. Nothing even in Willa Cather has the delicate pathos of this
passage in what later became "The Sleepers." By sensibility,
Whitman is as much a male lesbian as what fashionably we
term "gay." His poetry is panerotic, too comprehensive to be
subsumed by any so-called Homosexual Poetic. Like Shake-
speare's, Whitman's cosmos preludes Schopenhauer's and
Freud's. *Leaves of Grass*, and Shakespeare's plays and poems,
are in the domain of the will-to-live and the drives.

A brief while ago, I sorrowingly read the *New York Times*
obituary of the superb poet Anthony Hecht, and smiled grimly

at the obituary writer's literalization of Hecht's irony at describing himself as a Formalist poet. I once remarked to Hecht that our greatest Formalist poet was Walt Whitman, and met cheerful agreement. "Formalist poetry" is a redundancy: as our greatest American poet, Whitman is the supreme Formalist. His art is nuance, delicacy, inventiveness, intricate matching of sound to sense: we find in him, during his great decade of 1855 to 1865, the continuous prevalence of what John Hollander has termed "the trope of form." All poetic form, however newfangled, is necessarily metaphoric, a substitution of figurative for literal, of life for death. No poet makes it as impossible for us to know what is figurative and what is literal as Walt Whitman. His homoerotic yearnings plainly are authentic, if less pragmatic than his autoerotic adventures, but the masturbations enacted in "Song of Myself," "Spontaneous Me," and elsewhere seem on the borders of the metaphorical.

If we dwell in the United States, then Whitman indeed is our imaginative father and mother, even if, like myself, you have never composed a line of verse (it is for me a sacred threshold guarded by hungry demons). All of us long for transcendence, doubt such longings, and respond to Whitman's curious mingling of Emersonian Idealism and Epicurean Materialism. Whitman seems not to have read Emerson's later masterwork *The Conduct of Life*, where the goddess Nemesis presides over three scary essays: "Power," "Fate," and "Illusions," which leave us not much to celebrate. Whitman, when strongest, achieves an art in which celebration and elegy scarcely are distinguishable.

The revised "Song of Myself" was divided into fifty-two sections, presumably on the model of the weeks. Reading the poem undivided is a very different aesthetic experience, for me akin to the remarkable effect achieved by Horace Gregory, when in his anthology of consolatory poems he removed the section numbers from Tennyson's "In Memoriam," allowing it to run on as one continuous long poem. Something vital in the aesthetic *strangeness* of Whitman's epic diminishes when you end-stop it fifty-two times, even though you gain in the cognitive process of holding the self's grand chant all together.

The persona or mask of "Walt Whitman" never reconciled "my soul" and "the real me or me myself," as their only mode of coexistence was mutual "abasement," by Whitman's own testimony. But the persona allowed *Leaves of Grass* to get started and then to keep going until it ended with "Good-bye— and hail! my Fancy." "Walt Whitman" was (and is) an enabling Supreme Fiction, akin to the fiction of the snowy Leviathan Moby-Dick, or to Emily Dickinson's "Empress of Calvary." We have fictions aplenty these days but no one convincingly could proclaim their supremacy. Wallace Stevens's Snow Man and T. S. Eliot's Waste Land endure as negative fictions, and I myself remain sustained by Hart Crane's supreme fiction, a Platonized Brooklyn Bridge, metaphorically substituting for "Walt Whit- man." Our best living novelist is Philip Roth; our best poet, John Ashbery; our bourgeoning dramatist, Tony Kushner; yet I would hesitate to nominate Roth's Sabbath, Ashbery's "You," and Kushner's Roy Cohn as fictions eminently supreme, though someday they may seem so. Walt Whitman, James Wright lamented, "is now in America our country / Dead."

8

Is he, can he be, so long as our own higher culture survives? Emerson was our John the Baptist, but Whitman was our anointed one, hardly the American Jesus, but certainly the Amer- ican literary Christ. If we still have democratic vistas, they are those he sketched in his 1871 prose work of that title. Our new Gilded Age with its abuse of the underclass is little different from the one he denounced. His authority stems from yet another min- gling of figurative and literal, of "Walt Whitman" and the legiti- mate sayer: "I was the man, I suffered, I was there." He *was* there, the ministering Angel of the Washington, D.C., hospitals, as volunteer unpaid nurse and wound-dresser, self-appointed comforter of the maimed and dying soldiers of our most terrible of all wars. His service should haunt us still, as much the rightful myth of America as Father Abraham emancipating slaves. Who is more our vicarious atonement, President Lincoln or his elegist?

Leaves of Grass (1855) is the American Torah, the Teaching that inaugurates our scarcely secular Scripture. "There was a child went forth every day" and "the early lilacs became part of this child." The early lilacs returned to the exhausted wound-dresser of forty-six when he lamented his fallen leader in what moves me as the ultimate Formalist splendor of New World literature:

> In the dooryard fronting an old farm-house near the white-
> wash'd palings,
> Stands the lilac-bush tall-growing with heart-shaped leaves of
> rich green,
> With many a pointed blossom rising delicate, with the perfume
> strong I love,
> With every leaf a miracle—and from this bush in the dooryard,
> With delicate-color'd blossoms and heart-shaped leaves of rich
> green,
> A sprig with its flower I break.

The flowering sprig is what Whitman calls the "tally," the central emblem of his poetry from the first *Leaves of Grass* onward. As Whitman's image of voice, the "tally" is his central metaphor. A tally is a counting-up, but also a double or agreement. As a word, tally goes back to the Latin *talea* (twig, cutting, sprig), and in English initially meant a stick or cutting upon which you notched so as to keep score. First in English and then in the American language this acquired the sense of a sexual scoring. In much of the United States today, a "tallywoman" is an illicit girlfriend, and "tallywag" or "tallywhack" signifies male genitalia.

In the *Whispers of Heavenly Death* section of the final *Leaves of Grass* (1891–92), Whitman has the startling poem "Chanting the Square Deific" in which again he is "the Lord Christ":

> All sorrow, labor, suffering, I, tallying it, absorb in myself,
> Many times have I been rejected, taunted, put in prison, and
> crucified . . .

In what was to become section 25 of "Song of Myself," the tally is central:

Dazzling and tremendous how quick the sunrise would kill me,
If I could not now and always send sunrise out of me.

We also ascend dazzling and tremendous as the sun,
We found our own my soul in the calm and cool of the
    daybreak.

My voice goes after what my eyes cannot reach,
With the twirl of my tongue I encompass worlds and volumes
    of worlds.

Speech is the twin of my vision . . . . it is unequal to measure
    itself.

It provokes me forever,
It says sarcastically, Walt, you understand enough . . . . why
    don't you let it out then?

Come now I will not be tantalized . . . . you conceive too much
    of articulation,

Do you not know how the buds beneath you are folded?
Waiting in gloom protected by frost,
The dirt receding before my prophetical screams,
I underlying causes to balance them at last,
My knowledge my live parts . . . . it keeping tally with the
    meaning of things,
Happiness . . . . which whoever hears me let him or her set out
    in search of this day.

My final merit I refuse you . . . . I refuse putting from me the
    best I am.

Encompass worlds but never try to encompass me,
I crowd your noisiest talk by looking toward you.

Writing and talk do not prove me,
I carry the plenum of proof and every thing else in my face,
With the hush of my lips I confound the topmost skeptic.

"My knowledge my live parts . . . . it keeping tally with the meaning of things"—this is autosexual knowledge equated with the poem-making faculty. In "When Lilacs Last in the Dooryard Bloom'd" there is a marvelous juxtaposition of the two images of the tally: the sprig of lilac and the song of the hermit thrush (both surpassingly crucial also in *The Waste Land*). We pass from "A sprig with its flower I break" at the end of section 3 on to section 4:

> In the swamp in secluded recesses,
> A shy and hidden bird is warbling a song.
>
> Solitary the thrush,
> The hermit withdrawn to himself, avoiding the settlements,
> Sings by himself a song.
>
> Song of the bleeding throat,
> Death's outlet song of life, (for well dear brother I know,
> If thou wast not granted to sing, thou would'st surely die.)

The tally first appears in "Lilacs" as a verb, just before the hermit thrush sings Death's carol:

> And the charm of the carol rapt me,
> As I held as if by their hands my comrades in the night,
> And the voice of my spirit tallied the song of the bird.

After the song of Death, section 15 begins with a summoning: "To the tally of my soul." In section 16, the elegy's closure, "tallying" returns:

> I cease from my song for thee,
> From my gaze on thee in the west, fronting the west,
>   communing with thee,
> O comrade lustrous with silver face in the night.
>
> Yet each to keep and all, retrievements out of the night,
> The song, the wondrous chant of the gray-brown bird,

And the tallying chant, the echo arous'd in my soul,
With the lustrous and drooping star with the countenance full
    of woe,
With the holders holding my hand nearing the call of the bird,
Comrades mine and I in the midst, and their memory ever to
    keep for the dead I loved so well,
For the sweetest, wisest soul of all my days and lands—and this
    for his dear sake,
Lilac and star and bird twined with the chant of my soul,
There in the fragrant pines and the cedars dusk and dim.

"The tallying chant" is all of Whitman's greatest poetry of 1855–65, an echo which is what he can know of his own soul that hovers away from him out there in night, death, the mother, and the sea. Contrary to his self-affirmations, Whitman's highest art is Exodus, the metaphor of "get thee out from" Ur of the Chaldees or from Egypt into the promised land of a still undiscovered America.

9

What made *Leaves of Grass* (1855) possible? I am anything but a historicist, and burrowing beneath the American Renaissance will not account for the uniqueness of Walt Whitman (or of Emerson, Hawthorne, Melville, Thoreau, and the burgeoning James brothers William and Henry, or of Margaret Fuller, Frances Wright, and Alice James). My old acquaintance Malcolm Cowley, best friend of my mentor Kenneth Burke, credited a mystical experience of Whitman's. Though I have followed Gershom Scholem's fecund hint as to Whitman's analogue in Kabbalah, I do not regard Kabbalah as "Jewish mysticism" but as a mingling of Neoplatonist psychology and Gnostic mythology. While Walt keeps shouting "Kosmos!," I cannot locate New Age Cosmic Consciousness in him. Whitman is canny, endlessly evasive, a miracle of survival. Freud privately liked to call himself a Conquistador, and Emerson proudly termed himself an endless experimenter with no past at his back. In a literary sense, both idealized: Freud could not vanquish Shakespeare, and Emerson had Plutarch, Montaigne, Shakespeare, Goethe, Wordsworth, and Coleridge at his back.

Whitman had more than Emerson in his long foreground, but Emerson (rather like Goethe) constituted a culture in himself. Emerson was intrigued by the Swedenborgians' proclamations of the Newness, but like William Blake he shrugged off Swedenborg. Whitman's odd blend of Emersonianism and Epicureanism was all his own, yet had a forerunner in Shelley's curious mixture of Platonism and Lucretianism, and a descendant in Wallace Stevens's related eclecticism. Shelley and Stevens were skeptics, who qualified their affirmations. So ultimately did Whitman, and the 1855 *Leaves of Grass* already intimates the subtle limitations of its fiercely celebratory drives.

Though Whitman later denied it, Emerson made the first *Leaves of Grass* possible. The Concord Sage welcomed it, and never withdrew his endorsement, though he aged into many reservations, more even at the later Whitman's catalogings than at his sexual audacities (though to Emerson they seemed irrelevant proclamations). "Loyal at last" was Whitman's final judgment of his stance toward Emerson, who credited Whitman with the "Appalachian enlargement" of our literature. "As sane as the sun" was one of Whitman's final tributes to Emerson. My own favorite among Whitman's anecdotes is of his last visit to the then senile Emerson. The greatest of our poets so stationed his chair that he could stare fully at the benign countenance of his mentor, and each sat silently, Whitman in loving revery, and Emerson in the tragic solitude of an Alzheimer's victim. It was the final act in a grand drama of influence that started in the winter of 1854–55 and is still ongoing in our literary culture.

—Harold Bloom

Suggestions for Further Reading

1. The closest approach to a definitive text of Walt Whitman's poetry is the three-volume *Leaves of Grass: A Textual Variorum of the Printed Poems*, edited by Bradley, Blodgett, Golden, and White, New York University Press, 1980. But a really satisfactory complete *Leaves of Grass* does not yet exist. Besides this present celebratory reprint of the original 1855 text, devoted readers should acquaint themselves with the other great edition, the third of 1860, edited by Fredson Bowers, 1955, and also by Roy Harvey Pearce, 1961.

The crucial early notebook fragments of what was to develop into "Song of Myself" must be sought out in *Leaves of Grass*, edited by Emory Holloway in his *The Uncollected Poetry and Prose of Walt Whitman*, Vol. II, 1921. I have reprinted the seven fragments that seem to me most important in *Selected Poems*, the Library of America, 2003, edited by me.

2. Whitman's *Complete Prose Works* (1892) can be found in the Library of America *Whitman: Poetry and Prose*, 1982, edited by Justin Kaplan. *Memoranda During the War* is a useful supplement, edited by Peter Coviello, Oxford University Press, N.Y., 2004.

3. No single biography of Whitman has been wholly adequate, partly because much of our information is unreliable, while Whitman himself was sublimely evasive, and not only in the erotic sphere. I list the best we have, so far, in alphabetical order:

Justin Kaplan, *Walt Whitman: A Life*, 1980.
Jerome Loving, *Walt Whitman: The Song of Himself*, 1999.

Roy Morris, Jr., *The Better Angel: Whitman in the Civil War*, 2000.

David S. Reynolds, *Walt Whitman's America*, 1995.

4. Literary criticism of Walt Whitman always has been bad, and is worse than ever before. No one would now give us a study of Robert Browning, who seems to me Whitman's strongest poetic contemporary in the English language, that centers upon the great dramatic monologist's indubitable heterosexuality. But books and articles on Whitman's homoeroticism flood us, as though that in itself could be the basis for his aesthetic magnificence. I gathered together what I thought was the best criticism available by 1985 in *Walt Whitman: Modern Critical Views*, which I intend soon to revise and bring up to date. I suspect that the most illuminating criticism that ever will be written concerning Whitman will remain the final chapter of D. H. Lawrence's *Studies in Classic American Literature* (1923), despite Lawrence's violent ambivalence toward the precursor who had transformed him.

Leaves of Grass

The First (1855) Edition

Leaves

of

Grass.

———

Brooklyn, New York:
1855.

America does not repel the past or what it has produced under its forms or amid other politics or the idea of castes or the old religions . . . . accepts the lesson with calmness . . . is not so impatient as has been supposed that the slough still sticks to opinions and manners and literature while the life which served its requirements has passed into the new life of the new forms . . . perceives that the corpse is slowly borne from the eating and sleeping rooms of the house . . . perceives that it waits a little while in the door . . . that it was fittest for its days . . . that its action has descended to the stalwart and wellshaped heir who approaches . . . and that he shall be fittest for his days.

The Americans of all nations at any time upon the earth have probably the fullest poetical nature. The United States themselves are essentially the greatest poem. In the history of the earth hitherto the largest and most stirring appear tame and orderly to their ampler largeness and stir. Here at last is something in the doings of man that corresponds with the broadcast doings of the day and night. Here is not merely a nation but a teeming nation of nations. Here is action untied from strings necessarily blind to particulars and details magnificently moving in vast masses. Here is the hospitality which forever indicates heroes . . . . Here are the roughs and beards and space and ruggedness and nonchalance that the soul loves. Here the performance disdaining the trivial unapproached in the tremendous audacity of its crowds and groupings and the push of its perspective spreads with crampless and flowing breadth and showers its prolific and splendid extravagance. One sees it must indeed own the riches of the summer and winter, and need never be bankrupt while corn grows from the ground or the orchards drop apples or the bays contain fish or men beget children upon women.

Other states indicate themselves in their deputies . . . . but the genius of the United States is not best or most in its executives or legislatures, nor in its ambassadors or authors or colleges or churches or parlors, nor even in its newspapers or inventors . . . but always most in the common people. Their manners speech dress friendships—the freshness and candor of their physiognomy—the picturesque looseness of their carriage . . . their deathless attachment to freedom—their aversion to anything indecorous or soft or mean—the practical acknowledgment of the citizens of one state by the citizens of all other states—the fierceness of their roused resentment—their curiosity and welcome of novelty—their self-esteem and wonderful sympathy—their susceptibility to a slight—the air they have of persons who never knew how it felt to stand in the presence of superiors—the fluency of their speech—their delight in music, the sure symptom of manly tenderness and native elegance of soul . . . their good temper and openhandedness—the terrible significance of their elections—the President's taking off his hat to them not they to him—these too are unrhymed poetry. It awaits the gigantic and generous treatment worthy of it.

The largeness of nature of the nation were monstrous without a corresponding largeness and generosity of the spirit of the citizen. Not nature nor swarming states nor streets and steamships nor prosperous business nor farms nor capital nor learning may suffice for the ideal of man . . . nor suffice the poet. No reminiscences may suffice either. A live nation can always cut a deep mark and can have the best authority the cheapest . . . namely from its own soul. This is the sum of the profitable uses of individuals or states and of present action and grandeur and of the subjects of poets.—As if it were necessary to trot back generation after generation to the eastern records! As if the beauty and sacredness of the demonstrable must fall behind that of the mythical! As if men do not make their mark out of any times! As if the opening of the western continent by discovery and what has transpired since in North and South

America were less than the small theatre of the antique or the aimless sleepwalking of the middle ages! The pride of the United States leaves the wealth and finesse of the cities and all returns of commerce and agriculture and all the magnitude of geography or shows of exterior victory to enjoy the breed of fullsized men or one fullsized man unconquerable and simple.

The American poets are to enclose old and new for America is the race of races. Of them a bard is to be commensurate with a people. To him the other continents arrive as contributions . . . he gives them reception for their sake and his own sake. His spirit responds to his country's spirit . . . . he incarnates its geography and natural life and rivers and lakes. Mississippi with annual freshets and changing chutes, Missouri and Columbia and Ohio and Saint Lawrence with the falls and beautiful masculine Hudson, do not embouchure where they spend themselves more than they embouchure into him. The blue breadth over the inland sea of Virginia and Maryland and the sea off Massachusetts and Maine and over Manhattan bay and over Champlain and Erie and over Ontario and Huron and Michigan and Superior, and over the Texan and Mexican and Floridian and Cuban seas and over the seas off California and Oregon, is not tallied by the blue breadth of the waters below more than the breadth of above and below is tallied by him. When the long Atlantic coast stretches longer and the Pacific coast stretches longer he easily stretches with them north or south. He spans between them also from east to west and reflects what is between them. On him rise solid growths that offset the growths of pine and cedar and hemlock and liveoak and locust and chestnut and cypress and hickory and limetree and cottonwood and tuliptree and cactus and wildvine and tamarind and persimmon . . . . and tangles as tangled as any canebrake or swamp . . . . and forests coated with transparent ice and icicles hanging from the boughs and crackling in the wind . . . . and sides and peaks of mountains . . . . and pasturage sweet and free as savannah or upland or prairie . . . . with flights and songs and screams that answer those of the wildpigeon and highhold and orchard-oriole and coot and surf-duck and redshouldered-hawk and fish-hawk and white-ibis and indian-hen and cat-owl and water-pheasant and qua-bird and pied-sheldrake and blackbird and mockingbird and buzzard and condor and night-heron and eagle. To him the hereditary countenance descends both mother's and father's. To him enter the essences of the real things and past and present events—of the enormous diversity of temperature and agriculture and mines—the tribes of red aborigines—the weatherbeaten vessels entering new ports or making landings on rocky coasts—the first settlements north or south—the rapid stature and muscle—the haughty defiance of '76, and the war and peace and formation of the constitution . . . . the union always surrounded by blatherers and always calm and impregnable—the perpetual coming of immigrants—the wharfhem'd cities and superior marine—the unsurveyed interior—the loghouses and clearings and wild animals and hunters and trappers . . . . the free commerce—the fisheries and whaling and gold-digging—the endless gestation of new states—the convening of Congress every December, the members duly coming up from all climates and the uttermost parts . . . . the noble character of the young mechanics and of all free American workmen and work-women . . . . the general ardor and friendliness and enterprise—the perfect equality of the female with the male . . . . the large amativeness—the fluid movement of the population—the factories and mercantile life and laborsaving machinery—the Yankee swap—the New-York firemen and the target excursion—the southern plantation life—the character of the northeast and of the northwest and southwest—slavery and the tremulous spreading of hands to protect it, and the stern opposition to it which shall never cease till it ceases or the speaking of tongues and the moving of lips cease. For such the expression of the American poet is to be transcendent and new. It is to be indirect and not direct or descriptive or epic. Its quality goes through these to much more. Let the age and wars of other nations be chanted and their eras and characters be illustrated and that finish the verse. Not so the great psalm of the republic. Here the theme is creative and has vista. Here comes one among the well-beloved stonecutters and plans with decision and science and sees the solid and beautiful forms of the future where there are now no solid forms.

Of all nations the United States with veins full of poetical stuff most need poets and will doubtless have the greatest and use them the greatest. Their Presidents shall not be their common referee so much as their poets shall. Of all mankind the great poet is the equable man. Not in him but off from him things are grotesque or eccentric or fail of their sanity. Nothing out of its place is good and nothing in its place is bad. He bestows on every object or quality its fit proportions neither more nor less. He is the arbiter of the diverse and he is the key. He is the equalizer of his age and land . . . . he supplies what wants supplying and checks what wants checking. If peace is the routine out of him speaks the spirit of peace, large, rich, thrifty, building vast and populous cities, encouraging agriculture and the arts and commerce—lighting the study of man, the soul, immortality—federal, state or municipal government, marriage, health, freetrade, intertravel by land and sea . . . . nothing too close, nothing too far off . . . the stars not too far off. In war he is the most deadly force of the war. Who recruits him recruits horse and foot . . . he fetches parks of artillery the best that engineer ever knew. If the time becomes slothful and heavy he knows how to arouse it . . . he can make every word he speaks draw blood. Whatever stagnates in the flat of custom or obedience or legislation he never stagnates. Obedience does not master him, he masters it. High up out of reach he stands turning a concentrated light . . . he turns the pivot with his finger . . . he baffles the swiftest runners as he stands and easily overtakes and envelops them. The time straying toward infidelity and confections and persiflage he withholds by his steady faith . . . he spreads out his dishes . . . he offers the sweet firmfibred meat that grows men and women. His brain is the ultimate brain. He is no arguer . . . he is judgment. He judges not as the judge judges but as the sun falling around a helpless thing. As he sees the farthest he has the most faith. His thoughts are the hymns of the praise of things. In the talk on the soul and eternity and God off of his equal plane he is silent. He sees eternity less like a play with a prologue and denouement . . . . he sees eternity in men and women . . . he does not see men and women as dreams or dots. Faith is the antiseptic of the soul . . . it pervades the common people and preserves them . . . they never give up believing and expecting and trusting. There is that indescribable freshness and unconsciousness about an illiterate person that humbles and mocks the power of the noblest expressive genius. The poet sees for a certainty how one not a great artist may be just as sacred and perfect as the greatest artist. . . . . . The power to destroy or remould is freely used by him but never the power of attack. What is past is past. If he does not expose superior models and prove himself by every step he takes he is not what is wanted. The presence of the greatest poet conquers . . . not parleying or struggling or any prepared attempts. Now he has passed that way see after him! there is not left any vestige of despair or misanthropy or cunning or exclusiveness or the ignominy of a nativity or color or delusion of hell or the necessity of hell . . . . . and no man thenceforward shall be degraded for ignorance or weakness or sin.

The greatest poet hardly knows pettiness or triviality. If he breathes into any thing that was before thought small it dilates with the grandeur and life of the universe. He is a seer . . . . he is individual . . . he is complete in himself . . . . the others are as good as he, only he sees it and they do not. He is not one of the chorus . . . . he does not stop for any regulation . . . he is the president of regulation. What the eyesight does to the rest he does to the rest. Who knows the curious mystery of the eyesight? The other senses corroborate themselves, but this is removed from any proof but its own and foreruns the identities of the spiritual world. A single glance of it mocks all the investigations of man and all the instruments and books of the earth and all reasoning. What is marvellous? what is unlikely? what is impossible or baseless or vague? after you have once just opened the space of a peachpit and given audience to far and near and to the sunset and had all things enter with electric swiftness softly and duly without confusion or jostling or jam.

The land and sea, the animals fishes and birds, the sky of heaven and the orbs, the forests mountains and rivers, are not small themes . . . but folks expect of the poet to indicate more than the beauty and dignity which always attach to dumb real objects . . . . they expect him to indicate the path between reality and their souls. Men and women perceive the beauty well enough . . probably as well as he. The passionate tenacity of hunters, woodmen, early risers, cultivators of gardens and orchards and fields, the love of healthy women for the manly form, seafaring persons, drivers of horses, the passion for light and the open air, all is an old varied sign of the unfailing perception of beauty and of a residence of the poetic in outdoor people. They can never be assisted by poets to perceive . . . some may but they never can. The poetic quality is not marshalled in rhyme or uniformity or abstract addresses to things nor in melancholy complaints or good precepts, but is the life of these and much else and is in the soul. The profit of rhyme is that it drops seeds of a sweeter and more luxuriant rhyme, and of uniformity that it conveys itself into its own roots in the ground out of sight. The rhyme and uniformity of perfect poems show the free growth of metrical laws and bud from them as unerringly and loosely as lilacs or roses on a bush, and take shapes as compact as the shapes of chestnuts and oranges and melons and pears, and shed the perfume impalpable to form. The fluency and ornaments of the finest poems or music or orations or recitations are not independent but dependent. All beauty comes from beautiful blood and a beautiful brain. If the greatnesses are in conjunction in a man or woman it is enough . . . . the fact will prevail through the universe . . . . but the gaggery and gilt of a million years will not prevail. Who troubles himself about his ornaments or fluency is lost. This is what you shall do: Love the earth and sun and the animals, despise riches, give alms to every one that asks, stand up for the stupid and crazy, devote your income and labor to others, hate tyrants, argue not concerning God, have patience and indulgence toward the people, take off your hat to nothing known or unknown or to any man or number of men, go freely with powerful uneducated persons and with the young and with the mothers of families, read these leaves in the open air every season of every year of your life, re-examine all you have been told at school or church or in any book, dismiss whatever insults your own soul, and your very flesh shall be a great poem and have the richest fluency not only in its words but in the silent lines of its lips and face and between the lashes of your eyes and in every motion and joint of your body. . . . . . . The poet shall not spend his time in unneeded work. He shall know that the ground is always ready ploughed and manured . . . . others may not know it but he shall. He shall go directly to the creation. His trust shall master the trust of everything he touches . . . . and shall master all attachment.

The known universe has one complete lover and that is the greatest poet. He consumes an eternal passion and is indifferent which chance happens and which possible contingency of fortune or misfortune and persuades daily and hourly his delicious pay. What balks or breaks others is fuel for his burning progress to contact and amorous joy. Other proportions of the reception of pleasure dwindle to nothing to his proportions. All expected from heaven or from the highest he is rapport with in the sight of the daybreak or a scene of the winter woods or the presence of children playing or with his arm round the neck of a man or woman. His love above all love has leisure and expanse . . . . he leaves room ahead of himself. He is no irresolute or suspicious lover . . . he is sure . . . he scorns intervals. His experience and the showers and thrills are not for nothing. Nothing can jar him . . . . suffering and darkness cannot—death and fear cannot. To him complaint and jealousy and envy are corpses buried and rotten in the earth . . . . he saw them buried. The sea is not surer of the shore or the shore of the sea than he is of the fruition of his love and of all perfection and beauty.

The fruition of beauty is no chance of hit or miss . . . it is inevitable as life . . . . it is exact and plumb as gravitation. From the eyesight proceeds another eyesight and from the hearing proceeds another hearing and from the voice proceeds another voice eternally curious of the harmony of things with man. To these respond perfections not only in the committees that were supposed to stand for the rest but in the rest themselves just the same. These understand the law of perfection in masses and floods . . . that its finish is to each for itself and onward from itself . . . that it is profuse and impartial . . . that there is not a minute of the light or dark nor an acre of the earth or sea without it—nor any direction of the sky nor any trade or employment nor any turn of events. This is the reason that about the proper expression of beauty there is precision and balance . . . one part does not need to be thrust above another. The best singer is not the one who has the most lithe and powerful organ . . . the pleasure of poems is not in them that take the handsomest measure and similes and sound.

Without effort and without exposing in the least how it is done the greatest poet brings the spirit of any or all events and passions and scenes and persons some more and some less to bear on your individual character as you hear or read. To do this well is to compete with the laws that pursue and follow time. What is the purpose must surely be there and the clue of it must be there . . . . and the faintest indication is the indication of the best and then becomes the clearest indication. Past and present and future are not disjoined but joined. The greatest poet forms the consistence of what is to be from what has been and is. He drags the dead out of their coffins and stands them again on their feet . . . . he says to the past, Rise and walk before me that I may realize you. He learns the lesson . . . . he places himself where the future becomes present. The greatest poet does not only dazzle his rays over character and scenes and passions . . . he finally ascends and finishes all . . . he exhibits the pinnacles that no man can tell what they are for or what is beyond . . . . he glows a moment on the extremest verge. He is most wonderful in his last half-hidden smile or frown . . . by that flash of the moment of parting the one that sees it shall be encouraged or terrified afterwards for many years. The greatest poet does not moralize or make applications of morals . . . he knows the soul. The soul has that measureless pride which consists in never acknowledging any lessons but its own. But it has sympathy as measureless as its pride and the one balances the other and neither can stretch too far while it stretches in company with the other. The inmost secrets of art sleep with the twain. The greatest poet has lain close betwixt both and they are vital in his style and thoughts.

The art of art, the glory of expression and the sunshine of the light of letters is simplicity. Nothing is better than simplicity . . . . nothing can make up for excess or for the lack of

definiteness. To carry on the heave of impulse and pierce intel-
lectual depths and give all subjects their articulations are pow-
ers neither common nor very uncommon. But to speak in
literature with the perfect rectitude and insouciance of the
movements of animals and the unimpeachableness of the senti-
ment of trees in the woods and grass by the roadside is the flaw-
less triumph of art. If you have looked on him who has
achieved it you have looked on one of the masters of the artists
of all nations and times. You shall not contemplate the flight of
the graygull over the bay or the mettlesome action of the blood
horse or the tall leaning of sunflowers on their stalk or the ap-
pearance of the sun journeying through heaven or the appear-
ance of the moon afterward with any more satisfaction than
you shall contemplate him. The greatest poet has less a marked
style and is more the channel of thoughts and things without in-
crease or diminution, and is the free channel of himself. He
swears to his art, I will not be meddlesome, I will not have in
my writing any elegance or effect or originality to hang in the
way between me and the rest like curtains. I will have nothing
hang in the way, not the richest curtains. What I tell I tell for
precisely what it is. Let who may exalt or startle or fascinate or
soothe I will have purposes as health or heat or snow has and be
as regardless of observation. What I experience or portray shall
go from my composition without a shred of my composition.
You shall stand by my side and look in the mirror with me.

The old red blood and stainless gentility of great poets will
be proved by their unconstraint. A heroic person walks at his
ease through and out of that custom or precedent or authority
that suits him not. Of the traits of the brotherhood of writers
savans musicians inventors and artists nothing is finer than
silent defiance advancing from new free forms. In the need of
poems philosophy politics mechanism science behaviour, the
craft of art, an appropriate native grand-opera, shipcraft, or any
craft, he is greatest forever and forever who contributes the
greatest original practical example. The cleanest expression is
that which finds no sphere worthy of itself and makes one.

The messages of great poets to each man and woman are,
Come to us on equal terms, Only then can you understand us,

We are no better than you, What we enclose you enclose, What we enjoy you may enjoy. Did you suppose there could be only one Supreme? We affirm there can be unnumbered Supremes, and that one does not countervail another any more than one eyesight countervails another . . and that men can be good or grand only of the consciousness of their supremacy within them. What do you think is the grandeur of storms and dismemberments and the deadliest battles and wrecks and the wildest fury of the elements and the power of the sea and the motion of nature and of the throes of human desires and dignity and hate and love? It is that something in the soul which says, Rage on, Whirl on, I tread master here and everywhere, Master of the spasms of the sky and of the shatter of the sea, Master of nature and passion and death, And of all terror and all pain.

The American bards shall be marked for generosity and affection and for encouraging competitors . . They shall be kosmos . . without monopoly or secrecy . . glad to pass any thing to any one . . hungry for equals night and day. They shall not be careful of riches and privilege . . . . they shall be riches and privilege . . . . they shall perceive who the most affluent man is. The most affluent man is he that confronts all the shows he sees by equivalents out of the stronger wealth of himself. The American bard shall delineate no class of persons nor one or two out of the strata of interests nor love most nor truth most nor the soul most nor the body most . . . . and not be for the eastern states more than the western or the northern states more than the southern.

Exact science and its practical movements are no checks on the greatest poet but always his encouragement and support. The outset and remembrance are there . . there the arms that lifted him first and brace him best . . . . there he returns after all his goings and comings. The sailor and traveler . . the anatomist chemist astronomer geologist phrenologist spiritualist mathematician historian and lexicographer are not poets, but they are the lawgivers of poets and their construction underlies the structure of every perfect poem. No matter what rises or is uttered they sent the seed of the conception of it . . .

of them and by them stand the visible proofs of souls . . . . . always of their fatherstuff must be begotten the sinewy races of bards. If there shall be love and content between the father and the son and if the greatness of the son is the exuding of the greatness of the father there shall be love between the poet and the man of demonstrable science. In the beauty of poems are the tuft and final applause of science.

Great is the faith of the flush of knowledge and of the investigation of the depths of qualities and things. Cleaving and circling here swells the soul of the poet yet is president of itself always. The depths are fathomless and therefore calm. The innocence and nakedness are resumed . . . they are neither modest nor immodest. The whole theory of the special and supernatural and all that was twined with it or educed out of it departs as a dream. What has ever happened . . . . what happens and whatever may or shall happen, the vital laws enclose all . . . . they are sufficient for any case and for all cases . . . none to be hurried or retarded . . . . any miracle of affairs or persons inadmissible in the vast clear scheme where every motion and every spear of grass and the frames and spirits of men and women and all that concerns them are unspeakably perfect miracles all referring to all and each distinct and in its place. It is also not consistent with the reality of the soul to admit that there is anything in the known universe more divine than men and women.

Men and women and the earth and all upon it are simply to be taken as they are, and the investigation of their past and present and future shall be unintermitted and shall be done with perfect candor. Upon this basis philosophy speculates ever looking toward the poet, ever regarding the eternal tendencies of all toward happiness never inconsistent with what is clear to the senses and to the soul. For the eternal tendencies of all toward happiness make the only point of sane philosophy. Whatever comprehends less than that . . . whatever is less than the laws of light and of astronomical motion . . . or less than the laws that follow the thief the liar the glutton and the drunkard through this life and doubtless afterward . . . . . . or less than vast stretches of time or the slow formation of density or the patient upheaving of strata—is of no account. Whatever would put

God in a poem or system of philosophy as contending against some being or influence is also of no account. Sanity and ensemble characterise the great master . . . spoilt in one principle all is spoilt. The great master has nothing to do with miracles. He sees health for himself in being one of the mass . . . . he sees the hiatus in singular eminence. To the perfect shape comes common ground. To be under the general law is great for that is to correspond with it. The master knows that he is unspeakably great and that all are unspeakably great . . . . that nothing for instance is greater than to conceive children and bring them up well . . . that to be is just as great as to perceive or tell.

In the make of the great masters the idea of political liberty is indispensable. Liberty takes the adherence of heroes wherever men and women exist . . . . but never takes any adherence or welcome from the rest more than from poets. They are the voice and exposition of liberty. They out of ages are worthy the grand idea . . . . to them it is confided and they must sustain it. Nothing has precedence of it and nothing can warp or degrade it. The attitude of great poets is to cheer up slaves and horrify despots. The turn of their necks, the sound of their feet, the motions of their wrists, are full of hazard to the one and hope to the other. Come nigh them awhile and though they neither speak or advise you shall learn the faithful American lesson. Liberty is poorly served by men whose good intent is quelled from one failure or two failures or any number of failures, or from the casual indifference or ingratitude of the people, or from the sharp show of the tushes of power, or the bringing to bear soldiers and cannon or any penal statutes. Liberty relies upon itself, invites no one, promises nothing, sits in calmness and light, is positive and composed, and knows no discouragement. The battle rages with many a loud alarm and frequent advance and retreat . . . . the enemy triumphs . . . . the prison, the handcuffs, the iron necklace and anklet, the scaffold, garrote and leadballs do their work . . . . the cause is asleep . . . . the strong throats are choked with their own blood . . . . the young men drop their eyelashes toward the ground when they pass each other . . . . and is liberty gone out of that place? No never. When liberty goes it is not the first to go nor the second or third to go . . it waits for all the rest to go . . it is the last . . . When the memories of the old martyrs are faded utterly away . . . . when the large names of patriots are laughed at in the public halls from the lips of the orators . . . . when the boys are no more christened after the same but christened after tyrants and traitors instead . . . . when the laws of the free are grudgingly permitted and laws for informers and bloodmoney are sweet to the taste of the people . . . . when I and you walk abroad upon the earth stung with compassion at the sight of numberless brothers answering our equal friendship and calling no man master—and when we are elated with noble joy at the sight of slaves . . . . when the soul retires in the cool communion of the night and surveys its experience and has much extasy over the word and deed that put back a helpless innocent person into the gripe of the gripers or into any cruel inferiority . . . . when those in all parts of these states who could easier realize the true American character but do not yet—when the swarms of cringers, suckers, doughfaces, lice of politics, planners of sly involutions for their own preferment to city offices or state legislatures or the judiciary or congress or the presidency, obtain a response of love and natural deference from the people whether they get the offices or no . . . . when it is better to be a bound booby and rogue in office at a high salary than the poorest free mechanic or farmer with his hat unmoved from his head and firm eyes and a candid and generous heart . . . . and when servility by town or state or the federal government or any oppression on a large scale or small scale can be tried on without its own punishment following duly after in exact proportion against the smallest chance of escape . . . . or rather when all life and all the souls of men and women are discharged from any part of the earth—then only shall the instinct of liberty be discharged from that part of the earth.

As the attributes of the poets of the kosmos concentre in the real body and soul and in the pleasure of things they possess the superiority of genuineness over all fiction and romance. As they emit themselves facts are showered over with light . . . . the daylight is lit with more volatile light . . . . also the deep between the setting and rising sun goes deeper many fold. Each precise object or condition or combination or process exhibits a beauty . . . . the multiplication table its—old age its—the carpenter's trade its—the grand-opera its . . . . the hugehulled clean-shaped New-York clipper at sea under steam or full sail gleams with unmatched beauty . . . . the American circles and large harmonies of government gleam with theirs . . . . and the commonest definite intentions and actions with theirs. The poets of the kosmos advance through all interpositions and coverings and turmoils and stratagems to first principles. They are of use . . . . they dissolve poverty from its need and riches from its conceit. You large proprietor they say shall not realize or perceive more than any one else. The owner of the library is not he who holds a legal title to it having bought and paid for it. Any one and every one is owner of the library who can read the same through all the varieties of tongues and subjects and styles, and in whom they enter with ease and take residence and force toward paternity and maternity, and make supple and powerful and rich and large. . . . . These American states strong and healthy and accomplished shall receive no pleasure from violations of natural models and must not permit them. In paintings or mouldings or carvings in mineral or wood, or in the illustrations of books or newspapers, or in any comic or tragic prints, or in the patterns of woven stuffs or any thing to beautify rooms or furniture or costumes, or to put upon cornices or monuments or on the prows or sterns of ships, or to put anywhere before the human eye indoors or out, that which distorts honest shapes or which creates unearthly beings or places or contingencies is a nuisance and revolt. Of the human form especially it is so great it must never be made ridiculous. Of ornaments to a work nothing outre can be allowed . . but those ornaments can be allowed that conform to the perfect facts of the open air and that flow out of the nature of the work and come irrepressibly from it and are necessary to the completion of the work. Most works are most beautiful without ornament. . . Exaggerations will be revenged in human physiology. Clean and vigorous children are jetted and conceived only in those communities where the models of natural forms are public every day. . . . . . Great genius and the people of these states must never be demeaned to romances. As soon as histories are properly told there is no more need of romances.

The great poets are also to be known by the absence in them of tricks and by the justification of perfect personal candor. Then folks echo a new cheap joy and a divine voice leaping from their brains: How beautiful is candor! All faults may be forgiven of him who has perfect candor. Henceforth let no man of us lie, for we have seen that openness wins the inner and outer world and that there is no single exception, and that never since our earth gathered itself in a mass have deceit or subterfuge or prevarication attracted its smallest particle or the faintest tinge of a shade—and that through the enveloping wealth and rank of a state or the whole republic of states a sneak or sly person shall be discovered and despised . . . . and that the soul has never been once fooled and never can be fooled . . . . and thrift without the loving nod of the soul is only a fœtid puff . . . . and there never grew up in any of the continents of the globe nor upon any planet or satellite or star, nor upon the asteroids, nor in any part of ethereal space, nor in the midst of density, nor under the fluid wet of the sea, nor in that condition which precedes the birth of babes, nor at any time during the changes of life, nor in that condition that follows what we term death, nor in any stretch of abeyance or action afterward of vitality, nor in any process of formation or reformation anywhere, a being whose instinct hated the truth.

Extreme caution or prudence, the soundest organic health, large hope and comparison and fondness for women and children, large alimentiveness and destructiveness and causality, with a perfect sense of the oneness of nature and the propriety of the same spirit applied to human affairs . . these are called up of the float of the brain of the world to be parts of the greatest poet from his birth out of his mother's womb and from her birth out of her mother's. Caution seldom goes far enough. It has been thought that the prudent citizen was the citizen who applied himself to solid gains and did well for himself and his family and completed a lawful life without debt or crime. The greatest poet sees and admits these economies as he sees the economies of food and sleep, but has higher notions of prudence than to think he gives much when he gives a few slight attentions at the latch of the gate. The premises of the prudence of life are not the hospitality of it or the ripeness and harvest of it. Beyond the independence of a little sum laid aside for burial-money, and of a few clapboards around and shingles overhead on a lot of American soil owned, and the easy dollars that supply the year's plain clothing and meals, the melancholy prudence of the abandonment of such a great being as a man is to the toss and pallor of years of moneymaking with all their scorching days and icy nights and all their stifling deceits and underhanded dodgings, or infinitessimals of parlors, or shameless stuffing while others starve . . and all the loss of the bloom and odor of the earth and of the flowers and atmosphere and of the sea and of the true taste of the women and men you pass or have to do with in youth or middle age, and the issuing sickness and desperate revolt at the close of a life without elevation or naivete, and the ghastly chatter of a death without serenity or majesty, is the great fraud upon modern civilization and forethought, blotching the surface and system which civilization undeniably drafts, and moistening with tears the immense features it spreads and spreads with such velocity before the reached kisses of the soul. . . Still the right explanation remains to be made about prudence. The prudence of the mere wealth and respectability of the most esteemed life appears too faint for the eye to observe at all when little and large alike drop quietly aside at the thought of the prudence suitable for immortality. What is wisdom that fills the thinness of a year or seventy or eighty years to wisdom spaced out by ages and coming back at a certain time with strong reinforcements and rich presents and the clear faces of wedding-guests as far as you can look in every direction running gaily toward you? Only the soul is of itself . . . . all else has reference to what ensues. All that a person does or thinks is of consequence. Not a move can a man or woman make that affects him or her in a day or a month or any part of the direct lifetime or the hour of death but the same affects him or her onward afterward through the indirect lifetime. The indirect is always as great and real as the direct. The spirit receives from the body just as much as it gives to the body. Not one name of word or deed . . not of venereal sores or discolorations . . not the privacy of the onanist . . . not of the putrid veins of gluttons or rumdrinkers . . . not peculation or cunning or betrayal or murder . . no serpentine poison of those that seduce women . . not the foolish yielding of women . . not prostitution . . not of any depravity of young men . . not of the attainment of gain by discreditable means . . not any nastiness of appetite . . not any harshness of officers to men or judges to prisoners or fathers to sons or sons to fathers or husbands to wives or bosses to their boys . . not of greedy looks or malignant wishes . . . nor any of the wiles practised by people upon themselves . . . ever is or ever can be stamped on the programme but it is duly realized and returned, and that returned in further performances . . . and they returned again. Nor can the push of charity or personal force ever be any thing else than the profoundest reason, whether it brings arguments to hand or no. No specification is necessary . . to add or subtract or divide is in vain. Little or big, learned or unlearned, white or black, legal or illegal, sick or well, from the first inspiration down the windpipe to the last expiration out of it, all that a male or female does that is vigorous and benevolent and clean is so much sure profit to him or her in the unshakable order of the universe and through the whole scope of it forever. If the savage or felon is wise it is well . . . . if the greatest poet or savan is wise it is simply the same . . if the President or chief justice is wise it is the same . . . if the young mechanic or farmer is wise it is no more or less . . if the prostitute is wise it is no more nor less. The interest will come round . . all will come round. All the best actions of war and peace . . . all help given to relatives and strangers and the poor and old and sorrowful and young children and widows and the sick, and to all shunned persons . . all furtherance of fugitives and of the escape of slaves . . all the self-denial that stood steady and aloof on wrecks and saw others take the seats of the boats . . . all offering of substance or life for the good old cause, or for a friend's sake or opinion's sake . . . all pains of enthusiasts scoffed at by their neighbors . . all the vast sweet love and precious suffering of mothers . . . all honest men baffled in strifes recorded or

unrecorded . . . . all the grandeur and good of the few ancient
nations whose fragments of annals we inherit . . and all the
good of the hundreds of far mightier and more ancient nations
unknown to us by name or date or location . . . . all that was
ever manfully begun, whether it succeeded or no . . . . all that
has at any time been well suggested out of the divine heart of
man or by the divinity of his mouth or by the shaping of his
great hands . . and all that is well thought or done this day on
any part of the surface of the globe . . or on any of the wander-
ing stars or fixed stars by those there as we are here . . or that is
henceforth to be well thought or done by you whoever you are,
or by any one—these singly and wholly inured at their time and
inure now and will inure always to the identities from which
they sprung or shall spring . . . Did you guess any of them lived
only its moment? The world does not so exist . . no parts pal-
pable or impalpable so exist . . . no result exists now without
being from its long antecedent result, and that from its an-
tecedent, and so backward without the farthest mentionable spot
coming a bit nearer the beginning than any other spot. . . . .
Whatever satisfies the soul is truth. The prudence of the greatest
poet answers at last the craving and glut of the soul, is not con-
temptuous of less ways of prudence if they conform to its ways,
puts off nothing, permits no let-up for its own case or any case,
has no particular sabbath or judgment-day, divides not the liv-
ing from the dead or the righteous from the unrighteous, is sat-
isfied with the present, matches every thought or act by its
correlative, knows no possible forgiveness or deputed atone-
ment . . knows that the young man who composedly periled his
life and lost it has done exceeding well for himself, while the
man who has not periled his life and retains it to old age in
riches and ease has perhaps achieved nothing for himself worth
mentioning . . and that only that person has no great prudence
to learn who has learnt to prefer real longlived things, and fa-
vors body and soul the same, and perceives the indirect as-
suredly following the direct, and what evil or good he does
leaping onward and waiting to meet him again—and who in his
spirit in any emergency whatever neither hurries or avoids
death.

The direct trial of him who would be the greatest poet is to-day. If he does not flood himself with the immediate age as with vast oceanic tides . . . . . and if he does not attract his own land body and soul to himself and hang on its neck with incomparable love and plunge his semitic muscle into its merits and demerits . . . and if he be not himself the age transfigured . . . . and if to him is not opened the eternity which gives similitude to all periods and locations and processes and animate and inanimate forms, and which is the bond of time, and rises up from its inconceivable vagueness and infiniteness in the swimming shape of today, and is held by the ductile anchors of life, and makes the present spot the passage from what was to what shall be, and commits itself to the representation of this wave of an hour and this one of the sixty beautiful children of the wave—let him merge in the general run and wait his development. . . . . Still the final test of poems or any character or work remains. The prescient poet projects himself centuries ahead and judges performer or performance after the changes of time. Does it live through them? Does it still hold on untired? Will the same style and the direction of genius to similar points be satisfactory now? Has no new discovery in science or arrival at superior planes of thought and judgment and behaviour fixed him or his so that either can be looked down upon? Have the marches of tens and hundreds and thousands of years made willing detours to the right hand and the left hand for his sake? Is he beloved long and long after he is buried? Does the young man think often of him? and the young woman think often of him? and do the middleaged and the old think of him?

A great poem is for ages and ages in common and for all degrees and complexions and all departments and sects and for a woman as much as a man and a man as much as a woman. A great poem is no finish to a man or woman but rather a beginning. Has any one fancied he could sit at last under some due authority and rest satisfied with explanations and realize and be content and full? To no such terminus does the greatest poet bring . . . he brings neither cessation or sheltered fatness and ease. The touch of him tells in action. Whom he takes he takes with firm sure grasp into live regions previously unattained . . . .

thenceforward is no rest . . . . they see the space and ineffable sheen that turn the old spots and lights into dead vacuums. The companion of him beholds the birth and progress of stars and learns one of the meanings. Now there shall be a man cohered out of tumult and chaos . . . . the elder encourages the younger and shows him how . . . they two shall launch off fearlessly together till the new world fits an orbit for itself and looks unabashed on the lesser orbits of the stars and sweeps through the ceaseless rings and shall never be quiet again.

There will soon be no more priests. Their work is done. They may wait awhile . . perhaps a generation or two . . dropping off by degrees. A superior breed shall take their place . . . . the gangs of kosmos and prophets en masse shall take their place. A new order shall arise and they shall be the priests of man, and every man shall be his own priest. The churches built under their umbrage shall be the churches of men and women. Through the divinity of themselves shall the kosmos and the new breed of poets be interpreters of men and women and of all events and things. They shall find their inspiration in real objects today, symptoms of the past and future . . . . They shall not deign to defend immortality or God or the perfection of things or liberty or the exquisite beauty and reality of the soul. They shall arise in America and be responded to from the remainder of the earth.

The English language befriends the grand American expression . . . . it is brawny enough and limber and full enough. On the tough stock of a race who through all change of circumstances was never without the idea of political liberty, which is the animus of all liberty, it has attracted the terms of daintier and gayer and subtler and more elegant tongues. It is the powerful language of resistance . . . it is the dialect of common sense. It is the speech of the proud and melancholy races and of all who aspire. It is the chosen tongue to express growth faith self-esteem freedom justice equality friendliness amplitude prudence decision and courage. It is the medium that shall well nigh express the inexpressible.

No great literature nor any like style of behaviour or oratory or social intercourse or household arrangements or public institutions or the treatment by bosses of employed people, nor executive detail or detail of the army or navy, nor spirit of legislation or courts or police or tuition or architecture or songs or amusements or the costumes of young men, can long elude the jealous and passionate instinct of American standards. Whether or no the sign appears from the mouths of the people, it throbs a live interrogation in every freeman's and freewoman's heart after that which passes by or this built to remain. Is it uniform with my country? Are its disposals without ignominious distinctions? Is it for the evergrowing communes of brothers and lovers, large, well-united, proud beyond the old models, generous beyond all models? Is it something grown fresh out of the fields or drawn from the sea for use to me today here? I know that what answers for me an American must answer for any individual or nation that serves for a part of my materials. Does this answer? or is it without reference to universal needs? or sprung of the needs of the less developed society of special ranks? or old needs of pleasure overlaid by modern science and forms? Does this acknowledge liberty with audible and absolute acknowledgement, and set slavery at nought for life and death? Will it help breed one goodshaped and wellhung man, and a woman to be his perfect and independent mate? Does it improve manners? Is it for the nursing of the young of the republic? Does it solve readily with the sweet milk of the nipples of the breasts of the mother of many children? Has it too the old ever-fresh forbearance and impartiality? Does it look with the same love on the last born and on those hardening toward stature, and on the errant, and on those who disdain all strength of assault outside of their own?

The poems distilled from other poems will probably pass away. The coward will surely pass away. The expectation of the vital and great can only be satisfied by the demeanor of the vital and great. The swarms of the polished deprecating and reflectors and the polite float off and leave no remembrance. America prepares with composure and goodwill for the visitors that have sent word. It is not intellect that is to be their warrant and welcome. The talented, the artist, the ingenious, the editor, the statesman, the erudite . . they are not unappreciated . . they fall in their place and do their work. The soul of the nation also does its work. No disguise can pass on it . . no disguise can conceal from it. It rejects none, it permits all. Only toward as good as itself and toward the like of itself will it advance half-way. An individual is as superb as a nation when he has the qualities which make a superb nation. The soul of the largest and wealthiest and proudest nation may well go half-way to meet that of its poets. The signs are effectual. There is no fear of mistake. If the one is true the other is true. The proof of a poet is that his country absorbs him as affectionately as he has absorbed it.

LEAVES OF GRASS

[Song of Myself]

[1]

I celebrate myself,
And what I assume you shall assume,
For every atom belonging to me as good belongs to
    you.

I loafe and invite my soul,
I lean and loafe at my ease . . . . observing a spear of
    summer grass.

[2]

Houses and rooms are full of perfumes . . . . the shelves are
    crowded with perfumes,
I breathe the fragrance myself, and know it and like it,
The distillation would intoxicate me also, but I shall not
    let it.

The atmosphere is not a perfume . . . . it has no taste of
    the distillation . . . . it is odorless,
It is for my mouth forever . . . . I am in love with it,
I will go to the bank by the wood and become undisguised
    and naked,
I am mad for it to be in contact with me.

The smoke of my own breath,
Echoes, ripples, and buzzed whispers . . . . loveroot,
    silkthread, crotch and vine,
My respiration and inspiration . . . . the beating of my

heart . . . . the passing of blood and air through my
    lungs,   15
The sniff of green leaves and dry leaves, and of the shore
    and darkcolored sea-rocks, and of hay in the barn,
The sound of the belched words of my voice . . . . words
    loosed to the eddies of the wind,
A few light kisses . . . . a few embraces . . . . a reaching
    around of arms,
The play of shine and shade on the trees as the supple
    boughs wag,
The delight alone or in the rush of the streets, or along the
    fields and hillsides,   20
The feeling of health . . . . the full-noon trill . . . . the song
    of me rising from bed and meeting the sun.

Have you reckoned a thousand acres much? Have you
    reckoned the earth much?
Have you practiced so long to learn to read?
Have you felt so proud to get at the meaning of poems?

Stop this day and night with me and you shall possess the
    origin of all poems,   25
You shall possess the good of the earth and sun . . . . there
    are millions of suns left,
You shall no longer take things at second or third
    hand . . . . nor look through the eyes of the dead . . . .
    nor feed on the spectres in books,
You shall not look through my eyes either, nor take things
    from me,
You shall listen to all sides and filter them from yourself.

[3]

I have heard what the talkers were talking . . . . the talk of
    the beginning and the end,   30
But I do not talk of the beginning or the end.

There was never any more inception than there is now,
Nor any more youth or age than there is now;

And will never be any more perfection than there is
     now,
35 Nor any more heaven or hell than there is now.

Urge and urge and urge,
Always the procreant urge of the world.

Out of the dimness opposite equals advance . . . . Always
     substance and increase,
Always of knit of identity . . . . always distinction . . . .
     always a breed of life.

To elaborate is no avail . . . . Learned and unlearned feel
40   that it is so.

Sure as the most certain sure . . . . plumb in the uprights,
     well entretied, braced in the beams,
Stout as a horse, affectionate, haughty, electrical,
I and this mystery here we stand.

Clear and sweet is my soul . . . . and clear and sweet is all
     that is not my soul.

Lack one lacks both . . . . and the unseen is proved by the
45   seen,
Till that becomes unseen and receives proof in its turn.

Showing the best and dividing it from the worst, age vexes
     age,
Knowing the perfect fitness and equanimity of things,
     while they discuss I am silent, and go bathe and
     admire myself.

Welcome is every organ and attribute of me, and of any
     man hearty and clean,
Not an inch nor a particle of an inch is vile, and none
50   shall be less familiar than the rest.

I am satisfied . . . . I see, dance, laugh, sing;
As God comes a loving bedfellow and sleeps at my side all
    night and close on the peep of the day,
And leaves for me baskets covered with white towels
    bulging the house with their plenty,
Shall I postpone my acceptation and realization and
    scream at my eyes,
That they turn from gazing after and down the road,   55
And forthwith cipher and show me to a cent,
Exactly the contents of one, and exactly the contents of
    two, and which is ahead?

                            [4]
Trippers and askers surround me,
People I meet . . . . the effect upon me of my early life . . . .
    of the ward and city I live in . . . . of the nation,
The latest news . . . . discoveries, inventions, societies . . . .
    authors old and new,   60
My dinner, dress, associates, looks, business, compliments,
    dues,
The real or fancied indifference of some man or woman I
    love,
The sickness of one of my folks—or of myself . . . . or ill-
    doing . . . . or loss or lack of money . . . . or depressions
    or exaltations,
They come to me days and nights and go from me again,
But they are not the Me myself.   65

Apart from the pulling and hauling stands what I am,
Stands amused, complacent, compassionating, idle,
    unitary,
Looks down, is erect, bends an arm on an impalpable
    certain rest,
Looks with its sidecurved head curious what will come
    next,
Both in and out of the game, and watching and wondering
    at it.   70

Backward I see in my own days where I sweated through
    fog with linguists and contenders,
I have no mockings or arguments . . . . I witness and
    wait.

[5]
I believe in you my soul . . . . the other I am must not abase
    itself to you,
And you must not be abased to the other.

Loafe with me on the grass . . . . loose the stop from your
75   throat,
Not words, not music or rhyme I want . . . . not custom or
    lecture, not even the best,
Only the lull I like, the hum of your valved voice.

I mind how we lay in June, such a transparent summer
    morning;
You settled your head athwart my hips and gently turned
    over upon me,
And parted the shirt from my bosom-bone, and plunged
80   your tongue to my barestript heart,
And reached till you felt my beard, and reached till you
    held my feet.

Swiftly arose and spread around me the peace and joy and
    knowledge that pass all the art and argument of the
    earth;
And I know that the hand of God is the elderhand of my
    own,
And I know that the spirit of God is the eldest brother of
    my own,
And that all the men ever born are also my brothers . . . .
85   and the women my sisters and lovers,
And that a kelson of the creation is love;
And limitless are leaves stiff or drooping in the fields,
And brown ants in the little wells beneath them,

And mossy scabs of the wormfence, and heaped stones,
    and elder and mullen and pokeweed.

[6]
A child said, What is the grass? fetching it to me with full
    hands;   90
How could I answer the child? . . . . . . I do not know what
    it is any more than he.

I guess it must be the flag of my disposition, out of
    hopeful green stuff woven.

Or I guess it is the handkerchief of the Lord,
A scented gift and remembrancer designedly dropped,
Bearing the owner's name someway in the corners, that we
    may see and remark, and say Whose?   95

Or I guess the grass is itself a child . . . . the produced babe
    of the vegetation.

Or I guess it is a uniform hieroglyphic,
And it means, Sprouting alike in broad zones and narrow
    zones,
Growing among black folks as among white,
Kanuck, Tuckahoe, Congressman, Cuff, I give them the
    same, I receive them the same.   100

And now it seems to me the beautiful uncut hair of graves.

Tenderly will I use you curling grass,
It may be you transpire from the breasts of young men,
It may be if I had known them I would have loved them;
It may be you are from old people and from women, and
    from offspring taken soon out of their mothers' laps,   105
And here you are the mothers' laps.

This grass is very dark to be from the white heads of old
    mothers,

Darker than the colorless beards of old men,
Dark to come from under the faint red roofs of mouths.

110   O I perceive after all so many uttering tongues!
And I perceive they do not come from the roofs of mouths
    for nothing.

I wish I could translate the hints about the dead young
    men and women,
And the hints about old men and mothers, and the
    offspring taken soon out of their laps.

What do you think has become of the young and old men?
And what do you think has become of the women and
115   children?

They are alive and well somewhere;
The smallest sprout shows there is really no death,
And if ever there was it led forward life, and does not wait
    at the end to arrest it,
And ceased the moment life appeared.

120   All goes onward and outward . . . . and nothing collapses,
And to die is different from what any one supposed, and
    luckier.

[7]

Has any one supposed it lucky to be born?
I hasten to inform him or her it is just as lucky to die, and
    I know it.

I pass death with the dying, and birth with the new-
    washed babe. . . . and am not contained between my
    hat and boots,
And peruse manifold objects, no two alike, and every one
125   good,
The earth good, and the stars good, and their adjuncts all
    good.

I am not an earth nor an adjunct of an earth,
I am the mate and companion of people, all just as
    immortal and fathomless as myself;
They do not know how immortal, but I know.

Every kind for itself and its own . . . . for me mine male
    and female,   130
For me all that have been boys and that love women,
For me the man that is proud and feels how it stings to be
    slighted,
For me the sweetheart and the old maid . . . . for me
    mothers and the mothers of mothers,
For me lips that have smiled, eyes that have shed tears,
For me children and the begetters of children.   135

Who need be afraid of the merge?
Undrape. . . . you are not guilty to me, nor stale nor
    discarded,
I see through the broadcloth and gingham whether
    or no,
And am around, tenacious, acquisitive, tireless . . . . and
    can never be shaken away.

[8]
The little one sleeps in its cradle,   140
I lift the gauze and look a long time, and silently brush
    away flies with my hand.

The youngster and the redfaced girl turn aside up the
    bushy hill,
I peeringly view them from the top.

The suicide sprawls on the bloody floor of the bedroom,
It is so . . . . I witnessed the corpse . . . . there the pistol
    had fallen.   145

The blab of the pave . . . . the tires of carts and sluff of
    bootsoles and talk of the promenaders,

The heavy omnibus, the driver with his interrogating
    thumb, the clank of the shod horses on the granite
    floor,
The carnival of sleighs, the clinking and shouted jokes
    and pelts of snowballs;
The hurrahs for popular favorites . . . . the fury of roused
    mobs,
The flap of the curtained litter—the sick man inside,
150   borne to the hospital,
The meeting of enemies, the sudden oath, the blows and
    fall,
The excited crowd—the policeman with his star quickly
    working his passage to the centre of the crowd;
The impassive stones that receive and return so many
    echoes,
The souls moving along . . . . are they invisible while the
    least atom of the stones is visible?
What groans of overfed or half-starved who fall on the
155   flags sunstruck or in fits,
What exclamations of women taken suddenly, who hurry
    home and give birth to babes,
What living and buried speech is always vibrating
    here . . . . what howls restrained by decorum,
Arrests of criminals, slights, adulterous offers made,
    acceptances, rejections with convex lips,
I mind them or the resonance of them . . . . I come again
    and again.

[9]

160 The big doors of the country-barn stand open and ready,
The dried grass of the harvest-time loads the slow-drawn
    wagon,
The clear light plays on the brown gray and green
    intertinged,
The armfuls are packed to the sagging mow:
I am there . . . . I help . . . . I came stretched atop of the
    load,
165 I felt its soft jolts . . . . one leg reclined on the other,

I jump from the crossbeams, and seize the clover and
    timothy,
And roll head over heels, and tangle my hair full of wisps.

[10]
Alone far in the wilds and mountains I hunt,
Wandering amazed at my own lightness and glee,
In the late afternoon choosing a safe spot to pass the
    night,   170
Kindling a fire and broiling the freshkilled game,
Soundly falling asleep on the gathered leaves, my dog and
    gun by my side.

The Yankee clipper is under her three skysails . . . . she
    cuts the sparkle and scud,
My eyes settle the land . . . . I bend at her prow or shout
    joyously from the deck.

The boatmen and clamdiggers arose early and stopped for
    me,   175
I tucked my trowser-ends in my boots and went and had a
    good time,
You should have been with us that day round the chowder-
    kettle.

I saw the marriage of the trapper in the open air in the far-
    west . . . . the bride was a red girl,
Her father and his friends sat near by crosslegged and
    dumbly smoking . . . . they had moccasins to their feet
    and large thick blankets hanging from their shoulders;
On a bank lounged the trapper . . . . he was dressed mostly
    in skins . . . . his luxuriant beard and curls protected
    his neck,   180
One hand rested on his rifle . . . . the other hand held
    firmly the wrist of the red girl,
She had long eyelashes . . . . her head was bare . . . . her
    coarse straight locks descended upon her voluptuous
    limbs and reached to her feet.

The runaway slave came to my house and stopped outside,
I heard his motions crackling the twigs of the woodpile,
Through the swung half-door of the kitchen I saw him
185   limpsey and weak,
And went where he sat on a log, and led him in and
        assured him,
And brought water and filled a tub for his sweated body
        and bruised feet,
And gave him a room that entered from my own, and
        gave him some coarse clean clothes,
And remember perfectly well his revolving eyes and his
        awkwardness,
And remember putting plasters on the galls of his neck
190   and ankles;
He staid with me a week before he was recuperated and
        passed north,
I had him sit next me at table . . . . my firelock leaned in
        the corner.

[11]
Twenty-eight young men bathe by the shore,
Twenty-eight young men, and all so friendly,
195   Twenty-eight years of womanly life, and all so lonesome.

She owns the fine house by the rise of the bank,
She hides handsome and richly drest aft the blinds of the
        window.

Which of the young men does she like the best?
Ah the homeliest of them is beautiful to her.

200   Where are you off to, lady? for I see you,
You splash in the water there, yet stay stock still in your
        room.

Dancing and laughing along the beach came the twenty-
        ninth bather,
The rest did not see her, but she saw them and loved them.

The beards of the young men glistened with wet, it ran
    from their long hair,
Little streams passed all over their bodies.   205

An unseen hand also passed over their bodies,
It descended tremblingly from their temples and ribs.

The young men float on their backs, their white bellies
    swell to the sun . . . . they do not ask who seizes fast
    to them,
They do not know who puffs and declines with pendant
    and bending arch,
They do not think whom they souse with spray.   210

[12]
The butcher-boy puts off his killing-clothes, or sharpens
    his knife at the stall in the market,
I loiter enjoying his repartee and his shuffle and
    breakdown.

Blacksmiths with grimed and hairy chests environ the anvil,
Each has his main-sledge . . . . they are all out . . . . there
    is a great heat in the fire.

From the cinder-strewed threshold I follow their
    movements,   215
The lithe sheer of their waists plays even with their
    massive arms,
Overhand the hammers roll—overhand so slow—
    overhand so sure,
They do not hasten, each man hits in his place.

[13]
The negro holds firmly the reins of his four horses . . . .
    the block swags underneath on its tied-over chain,
The negro that drives the huge dray of the stoneyard . . . .
    steady and tall he stands poised on one leg on the
    stringpiece,   220

His blue shirt exposes his ample neck and breast and
    loosens over his hipband,
His glance is calm and commanding . . . . he tosses the
    slouch of his hat away from his forehead,
The sun falls on his crispy hair and moustache . . . . falls
    on the black of his polish'd and perfect limbs.

I behold the picturesque giant and love him . . . . and I do
    not stop there,
225 I go with the team also.

In me the caresser of life wherever moving . . . . backward
    as well as forward slueing,
To niches aside and junior bending.

Oxen that rattle the yoke or halt in the shade, what is that
    you express in your eyes?
It seems to me more than all the print I have read in my
    life.

My tread scares the wood-drake and wood-duck on my
230   distant and daylong ramble,
They rise together, they slowly circle around.
. . . . I believe in those winged purposes,
And acknowledge the red yellow and white playing
    within me,
And consider the green and violet and the tufted crown
    intentional;
And do not call the tortoise unworthy because she is not
235   something else,
And the mocking bird in the swamp never studied the
    gamut, yet trills pretty well to me,
And the look of the bay mare shames silliness out of me.

[14]
The wild gander leads his flock through the cool night,
Ya-honk! he says, and sounds it down to me like an
    invitation;

The pert may suppose it meaningless, but I listen closer,
I find its purpose and place up there toward the November
    sky.   240

The sharphoofed moose of the north, the cat on the
    housesill, the chickadee, the prairie-dog,
The litter of the grunting sow as they tug at her teats,
The brood of the turkeyhen, and she with her halfspread
    wings,
I see in them and myself the same old law.   245

The press of my foot to the earth springs a hundred
    affections,
They scorn the best I can do to relate them.

I am enamoured of growing outdoors,
Of men that live among cattle or taste of the ocean or
    woods,
Of the builders and steerers of ships, of the wielders of
    axes and mauls, of the drivers of horses,   250
I can eat and sleep with them week in and week out.

What is commonest and cheapest and nearest and easiest
    is Me,
Me going in for my chances, spending for vast returns,
Adorning myself to bestow myself on the first that will
    take me,
Not asking the sky to come down to my goodwill,   255
Scattering it freely forever.

[15]
The pure contralto sings in the organloft,
The carpenter dresses his plank . . . . the tongue of his
    foreplane whistles its wild ascending lisp,
The married and unmarried children ride home to their
    thanksgiving dinner,
The pilot seizes the king-pin, he heaves down with a
    strong arm,   260

The mate stands braced in the whaleboat, lance and
     harpoon are ready,
The duck-shooter walks by silent and cautious stretches,
The deacons are ordained with crossed hands at the altar,
The spinning-girl retreats and advances to the hum of the
     big wheel,
The farmer stops by the bars of a Sunday and looks at the
265   oats and rye,
The lunatic is carried at last to the asylum a confirmed
     case,
He will never sleep any more as he did in the cot in his
     mother's bedroom;
The jour printer with gray head and gaunt jaws works at
     his case,
He turns his quid of tobacco, his eyes get blurred with the
     manuscript;
270 The malformed limbs are tied to the anatomist's table,
What is removed drops horribly in a pail;
The quadroon girl is sold at the stand . . . . the drunkard
     nods by the barroom stove,
The machinist rolls up his sleeves . . . . the policeman
     travels his beat . . . . the gatekeeper marks who pass,
The young fellow drives the express-wagon . . . . I love
     him though I do not know him;
The half-breed straps on his light boots to compete in the
275   race,
The western turkey-shooting draws old and young . . . .
     some lean on their rifles, some sit on logs,
Out from the crowd steps the marksman and takes his
     position and levels his piece;
The groups of newly-come immigrants cover the wharf or
     levee,
The woollypates hoe in the sugarfield, the overseer views
     them from his saddle;
The bugle calls in the ballroom, the gentlemen run for
280   their partners, the dancers bow to each other;
The youth lies awake in the cedar-roofed garret and harks
     to the musical rain,

The Wolverine sets traps on the creek that helps fill the
    Huron,
The reformer ascends the platform, he spouts with his
    mouth and nose,
The company returns from its excursion, the darkey
    brings up the rear and bears the well-riddled target,
The squaw wrapt in her yellow-hemmed cloth is offering
    moccasins and beadbags for sale,   285
The connoisseur peers along the exhibition-gallery with
    halfshut eyes bent sideways,
The deckhands make fast the steamboat, the plank is
    thrown for the shoregoing passengers,
The young sister holds out the skein, the elder sister
    winds it off in a ball and stops now and then for the
    knots,
The one-year wife is recovering and happy, a week ago
    she bore her first child,
The cleanhaired Yankee girl works with her sewing-
    machine or in the factory or mill,   290
The nine months' gone is in the parturition chamber, her
    faintness and pains are advancing;
The pavingman leans on his twohanded rammer—the
    reporter's lead flies swiftly over the notebook—the
    signpainter is lettering with red and gold,
The canal-boy trots on the towpath—the bookkeeper
    counts at his desk—the shoemaker waxes his thread,
The conductor beats time for the band and all the
    performers follow him,
The child is baptised—the convert is making the first
    professions,   295
The regatta is spread on the bay . . . . how the white sails
    sparkle!
The drover watches his drove, he sings out to them that
    would stray,
The pedlar sweats with his pack on his back—the
    purchaser higgles about the odd cent,
The camera and plate are prepared, the lady must sit for
    her daguerreotype,

The bride unrumples her white dress, the minutehand of
300   the clock moves slowly,
The opium eater reclines with rigid head and just-opened
      lips,
The prostitute draggles her shawl, her bonnet bobs on her
      tipsy and pimpled neck,
The crowd laugh at her blackguard oaths, the men jeer
      and wink to each other,
(Miserable! I do not laugh at your oaths nor jeer you,)
The President holds a cabinet council, he is surrounded by
305   the great secretaries,
On the piazza walk five friendly matrons with twined
      arms;
The crew of the fish-smack pack repeated layers of
      halibut in the hold,
The Missourian crosses the plains toting his wares and his
      cattle,
The fare-collector goes through the train—he gives notice
      by the jingling of loose change,
The floormen are laying the floor—the tinners are tinning
310   the roof—the masons are calling for mortar,
In single file each shouldering his hod pass onward the
      laborers;
Seasons pursuing each other the indescribable crowd is
      gathered . . . . it is the Fourth of July . . . . what
      salutes of cannon and small arms!
Seasons pursuing each other the plougher ploughs and
      the mower mows and the wintergrain falls in the
      ground;
Off on the lakes the pikefisher watches and waits by the
      hole in the frozen surface,
The stumps stand thick round the clearing, the squatter
315   strikes deep with his axe,
The flatboatmen make fast toward dusk near the
      cottonwood or pekantrees,
The coon-seekers go now through the regions of the Red
      river, or through those drained by the Tennessee, or
      through those of the Arkansas,

The torches shine in the dark that hangs on the
    Chattahoochee or Altamahaw;
Patriarchs sit at supper with sons and grandsons and great
    grandsons around them,
In walls of adobie, in canvas tents, rest hunters and
    trappers after their day's sport.   320

The city sleeps and the country sleeps,
The living sleep for their time . . . . the dead sleep for their
    time,
The old husband sleeps by his wife and the young
    husband sleeps by his wife;
And these one and all tend inward to me, and I tend
    outward to them,
And such as it is to be of these more or less I am.   325

[16]
I am of old and young, of the foolish as much as the
    wise,
Regardless of others, ever regardful of others,
Maternal as well as paternal, a child as well as a man,
Stuffed with the stuff that is coarse, and stuffed with the
    stuff that is fine,
One of the great nations, the nation of many nations—the
    smallest the same and the largest the same,   330
A southerner soon as a northerner, a planter nonchalant
    and hospitable,
A Yankee bound my own way . . . . ready for trade . . . .
    my joints the limberest joints on earth and the sternest
    joints on earth,
A Kentuckian walking the vale of the Elkhorn in my
    deerskin leggings,
A boatman over the lakes or bays or along coasts . . . . a
    Hoosier, a Badger, a Buckeye,
A Louisianian or Georgian, a poke-easy from sandhills
    and pines,   335
At home on Canadian snowshoes or up in the bush, or
    with fishermen off Newfoundland,

At home in the fleet of iceboats, sailing with the rest and
    tacking,
At home on the hills of Vermont or in the woods of
    Maine or the Texan ranch,
Comrade of Californians . . . . comrade of free
    northwesterners, loving their big proportions,
Comrade of raftsmen and coalmen—comrade of all who
340   shake hands and welcome to drink and meat;
A learner with the simplest, a teacher of the thoughtfulest,
A novice beginning experient of myriads of seasons,
Of every hue and trade and rank, of every caste and
    religion,
Not merely of the New World but of Africa Europe or
    Asia . . . . a wandering savage,
A farmer, mechanic, or artist . . . . a gentleman, sailor,
345   lover or quaker,
A prisoner, fancy-man, rowdy, lawyer, physician or
    priest.

I resist anything better than my own diversity,
And breathe the air and leave plenty after me,
And am not stuck up, and am in my place.

350 The moth and the fisheggs are in their place,
The suns I see and the suns I cannot see are in their place,
The palpable is in its place and the impalpable is in its
    place.

[17]
These are the thoughts of all men in all ages and lands,
    they are not original with me,
If they are not yours as much as mine they are nothing or
    next to nothing,
355 If they do not enclose everything they are next to nothing,
If they are not the riddle and the untying of the riddle
    they are nothing,
If they are not just as close as they are distant they are
    nothing.

This is the grass that grows wherever the land is and the
    water is,
This is the common air that bathes the globe.

This is the breath of laws and songs and behaviour,   360
This is the tasteless water of souls . . . . this is the true
    sustenance,
It is for the illiterate . . . . it is for the judges of the supreme
    court . . . . it is for the federal capitol and the state
    capitols,
It is for the admirable communes of literary men and
    composers and singers and lecturers and engineers and
    savans,
It is for the endless races of working people and farmers
    and seamen.

[18]
This is the trill of a thousand clear cornets and scream of
    the octave flute and strike of triangles.   365
I play not a march for victors only . . . . I play great
    marches for conquered and slain persons.

Have you heard that it was good to gain the day?
I also say it is good to fall . . . . battles are lost in the same
    spirit in which they are won.

I sound triumphal drums for the dead . . . . I fling through
    my embouchures the loudest and gayest music to them,
Vivas to those who have failed, and to those whose war-
    vessels sank in the sea, and those themselves who sank
    in the sea,   370
And to all generals that lost engagements, and all
    overcome heroes, and the numberless unknown heroes
    equal to the greatest heroes known.

[19]
This is the meal pleasantly set . . . . this is the meat and
    drink for natural hunger,

It is for the wicked just the same as the righteous I
    make appointments with all,
I will not have a single person slighted or left away,
The keptwoman and sponger and thief are hereby
    invited . . . . the heavy-lipped slave is invited. . . . the
375   venerealee is invited,
There shall be no difference between them and the rest.

This is the press of a bashful hand . . . . this is the float
    and odor of hair,
This is the touch of my lips to yours . . . . this is the
    murmur of yearning,
This is the far-off depth and height reflecting my own face,
380 This is the thoughtful merge of myself and the outlet again.

Do you guess I have some intricate purpose?
Well I have . . . . for the April rain has, and the mica on
    the side of a rock has.

Do you take it I would astonish?
Does the daylight astonish? or the early redstart
    twittering through the woods?
385 Do I astonish more than they?

This hour I tell things in confidence,
I might not tell everybody but I will tell you.

[20]
Who goes there! hankering, gross, mystical, nude?
How is it I extract strength from the beef I eat?

390 What is a man anyhow? What am I? and what are you?
All I mark as my own you shall offset it with your own,
Else it were time lost listening to me.

I do not snivel that snivel the world over,
That months are vacuums and the ground but wallow and
    filth,

That life is a suck and a sell, and nothing remains at the
    end but threadbare crape and tears.   395

Whimpering and truckling fold with powders for
    invalids . . . . conformity goes to the fourth-removed,
I cock my hat as I please indoors or out.

Shall I pray? Shall I venerate and be ceremonious?
I have pried through the strata and analyzed to a hair,
And counselled with doctors and calculated close and
    found no sweeter fat than sticks to my own bones.   400

In all people I see myself, none more and not one a
    barleycorn less,
And the good or bad I say of myself I say of them.

And I know I am solid and sound,
To me the converging objects of the universe perpetually
    flow,
All are written to me, and I must get what the writing
    means.   405

And I know I am deathless,
I know this orbit of mine cannot be swept by a carpenter's
    compass,
I know I shall not pass like a child's carlacue cut with a
    burnt stick at night.

I know I am august,
I do not trouble my spirit to vindicate itself or be
    understood,   410
I see that the elementary laws never apologize,
I reckon I behave no prouder than the level I plant my
    house by after all.

I exist as I am, that is enough,
If no other in the world be aware I sit content,
And if each and all be aware I sit content.   415

One world is aware, and by far the largest to me, and that
    is myself,
And whether I come to my own today or in ten thousand
    or ten million years,
I can cheerfully take it now, or with equal cheerfulness I
    can wait.

My foothold is tenoned and mortised in granite,
420 I laugh at what you call dissolution,
And I know the amplitude of time.

[21]
I am the poet of the body,
And I am the poet of the soul.

The pleasures of heaven are with me, and the pains of hell
    are with me,
The first I graft and increase upon myself . . . . the latter I
425   translate into a new tongue.

I am the poet of the woman the same as the man,
And I say it is as great to be a woman as to be a man,
And I say there is nothing greater than the mother of men.

I chant a new chant of dilation or pride,
430 We have had ducking and deprecating about enough,
I show that size is only development.

Have you outstript the rest? Are you the President?
It is a trifle . . . . they will more than arrive there every one,
    and still pass on.

I am he that walks with the tender and growing night;
I call to the earth and sea half-held by the night.

435 Press close barebosomed night! Press close magnetic
    nourishing night!

Night of south winds! Night of the large few stars!
Still nodding night! Mad naked summer night!

Smile O voluptuous coolbreathed earth!
Earth of the slumbering and liquid trees!   440
Earth of departed sunset! Earth of the mountains misty-
    topt!
Earth of the vitreous pour of the full moon just tinged
    with blue!
Earth of shine and dark mottling the tide of the river!
Earth of the limpid gray of clouds brighter and clearer for
    my sake!
Far-swooping elbowed earth! Rich apple-blossomed earth!   445
Smile, for your lover comes!

Prodigal! you have given me love! . . . . therefore I to you
    give love!
O unspeakable passionate love!

Thruster holding me tight and that I hold tight!
We hurt each other as the bridegroom and the bride hurt
    each other.   450

[22]
You sea! I resign myself to you also . . . . I guess what you
    mean,
I behold from the beach your crooked inviting fingers,
I believe you refuse to go back without feeling of me;
We must have a turn together . . . . I undress . . . . hurry me
    out of sight of the land,
Cushion me soft . . . . rock me in billowy drowse,   455
Dash me with amorous wet . . . . I can repay you.

Sea of stretched ground-swells!
Sea breathing broad and convulsive breaths!
Sea of the brine of life! Sea of unshovelled and always-
    ready graves!

460 Howler and scooper of storms! Capricious and dainty sea!
     I am integral with you . . . . I too am of one phase and of
        all phases.

     Partaker of influx and efflux . . . . extoller of hate and
        conciliation,
     Extoller of amies and those that sleep in each others' arms.

     I am he attesting sympathy;
     Shall I make my list of things in the house and skip the
465   house that supports them?

     I am the poet of commonsense and of the demonstrable
        and of immortality;
     And am not the poet of goodness only . . . . I do not
        decline to be the poet of wickedness also.

     Washes and razors for foofoos . . . . for me freckles and a
        bristling beard.

     What blurt is it about virtue and about vice?
     Evil propels me, and reform of evil propels me . . . . I stand
470   indifferent,
     My gait is no faultfinder's or rejecter's gait,
     I moisten the roots of all that has grown.

     Did you fear some scrofula out of the unflagging
        pregnancy?
     Did you guess the celestial laws are yet to be worked over
        and rectified?

     I step up to say that what we do is right and what we
475   affirm is right . . . . and some is only the ore of right,
     Witnesses of us . . . . one side a balance and the antipodal
        side a balance,
     Soft doctrine as steady help as stable doctrine,
     Thoughts and deeds of the present our rouse and early
        start.

This minute that comes to me over the past decillions,
There is no better than it and now.   480

What behaved well in the past or behaves well today is
    not such a wonder,
The wonder is always and always how there can be a
    mean man or an infidel.

[23]
Endless unfolding of words of ages!
And mine a word of the modern . . . . a word en masse.

A word of the faith that never balks,   485
One time as good as another time . . . . here or
    henceforward it is all the same to me.

A word of reality . . . . materialism first and last imbuing.

Hurrah for positive science! Long live exact
    demonstration!
Fetch stonecrop and mix it with cedar and branches of
    lilac;
This is the lexicographer or chemist . . . . this made a
    grammar of the old cartouches,   490
These mariners put the ship through dangerous unknown
    seas,
This is the geologist, and this works with the scalpel, and
    this is a mathematician.

Gentlemen I receive you, and attach and clasp hands with
    you,
The facts are useful and real . . . . they are not my
    dwelling . . . . I enter by them to an area of the
    dwelling.

I am less the reminder of property or qualities, and more
    the reminder of life,   495
And go on the square for my own sake and for other's sake,

And make short account of neuters and geldings, and
   favor men and women fully equipped,
And beat the gong of revolt, and stop with fugitives and
   them that plot and conspire.

[24]
Walt Whitman, an American, one of the roughs, a kosmos,
Disorderly fleshy and sensual . . . . eating drinking and
500   breeding,
No sentimentalist . . . . no stander above men and women or
   apart from them . . . . no more modest than immodest.

Unscrew the locks from the doors!
Unscrew the doors themselves from their jambs!

Whoever degrades another degrades me . . . . and whatever
   is done or said returns at last to me,
505   And whatever I do or say I also return.

Through me the afflatus surging and surging . . . . through
   me the current and index.

I speak the password primeval . . . . I give the sign of
   democracy;
By God! I will accept nothing which all cannot have their
   counterpart of on the same terms.

Through me many long dumb voices,
510   Voices of the interminable generations of slaves,
Voices of prostitutes and of deformed persons,
Voices of the diseased and despairing, and of thieves and
   dwarfs,
Voices of cycles of preparation and accretion,
And of the threads that connect the stars—and of wombs,
   and of the fatherstuff,
515   And of the rights of them the others are down upon,
Of the trivial and flat and foolish and despised,
Of fog in the air and beetles rolling balls of dung.

Through me forbidden voices,
Voices of sexes and lusts . . . . voices veiled, and I remove
    the veil,
Voices indecent by me clarified and transfigured.   520

I do not press my finger across my mouth,
I keep as delicate around the bowels as around the head
    and heart,
Copulation is no more rank to me than death is.

I believe in the flesh and the appetites,
Seeing hearing and feeling are miracles, and each part and
    tag of me is a miracle.   525

Divine am I inside and out, and I make holy whatever I
    touch or am touched from;
The scent of these arm-pits is aroma finer than prayer,
This head is more than churches or bibles or creeds.

If I worship any particular thing it shall be some of the
    spread of my body;   530
Translucent mould of me it shall be you,
Shaded ledges and rests, firm masculine coulter, it shall be
    you,
Whatever goes to the tilth of me it shall be you,
You my rich blood, your milky stream pale strippings of
    my life;
Breast that presses against other breasts it shall be you,
My brain it shall be your occult convolutions,   535
Root of washed sweet-flag, timorous pond-snipe, nest of
    guarded duplicate eggs, it shall be you,
Mixed tussled hay of head and beard and brawn it shall
    be you,
Trickling sap of maple, fibre of manly wheat, it shall be
    you;
Sun so generous it shall be you,
Vapors lighting and shading my face it shall be you,   540
You sweaty brooks and dews it shall be you,

Winds whose soft-tickling genitals rub against me it shall
 be you,
Broad muscular fields, branches of liveoak, loving lounger
 in my winding paths, it shall be you,
Hands I have taken, face I have kissed, mortal I have ever
 touched, it shall be you.

I dote on myself . . . . there is that lot of me, and all so
545 luscious,
Each moment and whatever happens thrills me with joy.

I cannot tell how my ankles bend . . . . nor whence the
 cause of my faintest wish,
Nor the cause of the friendship I emit . . . . nor the cause
 of the friendship I take again.

To walk up my stoop is unaccountable . . . . I pause to
 consider if it really be,
That I eat and drink is spectacle enough for the great
550 authors and schools,
A morning-glory at my window satisfies me more than the
 metaphysics of books.

To behold the daybreak!
The little light fades the immense and diaphanous
 shadows,
The air tastes good to my palate.

Hefts of the moving world at innocent gambols, silently
555 rising, freshly exuding,
Scooting obliquely high and low.

Something I cannot see puts upward libidinous
 prongs,
Seas of bright juice suffuse heaven.

The earth by the sky staid with . . . . the daily close of
 their junction,

The heaved challenge from the east that moment over my
    head, 560
The mocking taunt, See then whether you shall be master!

[25]

Dazzling and tremendous how quick the sunrise would
    kill me,
If I could not now and always send sunrise out of me.

We also ascend dazzling and tremendous as the sun,
We found our own my soul in the calm and cool of the
    daybreak. 565

My voice goes after what my eyes cannot reach,
With the twirl of my tongue I encompass worlds and
    volumes of worlds.

Speech is the twin of my vision . . . . it is unequal to
    measure itself.

It provokes me forever,
It says sarcastically, Walt, you understand enough . . . .
    why don't you let it out then? 570

Come now I will not be tantalized . . . . you conceive too
    much of articulation.

Do you not know how the buds beneath are folded?
Waiting in gloom protected by frost,
The dirt receding before my prophetical screams,
I underlying causes to balance them at last, 575
My knowledge my live parts . . . . it keeping tally with the
    meaning of things,
Happiness . . . . which whoever hears me let him or her set
    out in search of this day.

My final merit I refuse you . . . . I refuse putting from me
    the best I am.

Encompass worlds but never try to encompass me,
580   I crowd your noisiest talk by looking toward you.

Writing and talk do not prove me,
I carry the plenum of proof and every thing else in my
        face,
With the hush of my lips I confound the topmost
        skeptic.

[26]

I think I will do nothing for a long time but listen,
And accrue what I hear into myself . . . . and let sounds
585   contribute toward me.

I hear the bravuras of birds . . . . the bustle of growing
        wheat . . . . gossip of flames . . . . clack of sticks
        cooking my meals.

I hear the sound of the human voice . . . . a sound I love,
I hear all sounds as they are tuned to their uses . . . .
        sounds of the city and sounds out of the city . . . .
        sounds of the day and night;
Talkative young ones to those that like them . . . . the
        recitative of fish-pedlars and fruit-pedlars . . . . the
        loud laugh of workpeople at their meals,
The angry base of disjointed friendship . . . . the faint
590   tones of the sick,
The judge with hands tight to the desk, his shaky lips
        pronouncing a death-sentence,
The heave'e'yo of stevedores unlading ships by the
        wharves . . . . the refrain of the anchor-lifters;
The ring of alarm-bells . . . . the cry of fire . . . . the whirr
        of swift-streaking engines and hose-carts with
        premonitory tinkles and colored lights,
The steam-whistle . . . . the solid roll of the train of
        approaching cars;
The slow-march played at night at the head of the
595   association,

They go to guard some corpse . . . . the flag-tops are
    draped with black muslin.

I hear the violincello or man's heart complaint,
And hear the keyed cornet or else the echo of sunset.

I hear the chorus . . . . it is a grand-opera . . . . this indeed
    is music!

A tenor large and fresh as the creation fills me,   600
The orbic flex of his mouth is pouring and filling me full.

I hear the trained soprano . . . . she convulses me like the
    climax of my love-grip;
The orchestra whirls me wider than Uranus flies,
It wrenches unnamable ardors from my breast,
It throbs me to gulps of the farthest down horror,   605
It sails me . . . . I dab with bare feet . . . . they are licked
    by the indolent waves,
I am exposed . . . . cut by bitter and poisoned hail,
Steeped amid honeyed morphine . . . . my windpipe
    squeezed in the fakes of death,
Let up again to feel the puzzle of puzzles,
And that we call Being.   610

[27]
To be in any form, what is that?
If nothing lay more developed the quahaug and its callous
    shell were enough.

Mine is no callous shell,
I have instant conductors all over me whether I pass or
    stop,
They seize every object and lead it harmlessly through me. 615

I merely stir, press, feel with my fingers, and am happy,
To touch my person to some one else's is about as much as
    I can stand.

[28]

Is this then a touch? . . . . quivering me to a new identity,
Flames and ether making a rush for my veins,
Treacherous tip of me reaching and crowding to help
620   them,
My flesh and blood playing out lightning, to strike what is
      hardly different from myself,
On all sides prurient provokers stiffening my limbs,
Straining the udder of my heart for its withheld drip,
Behaving licentious toward me, taking no denial,
625 Depriving me of my best as for a purpose,
Unbuttoning my clothes and holding me by the bare waist,
Deluding my confusion with the calm of the sunlight and
      pasture fields,
Immodestly sliding the fellow-senses away,
They bribed to swap off with touch, and go and graze at
      the edges of me,
No consideration, no regard for my draining strength or
630   my anger,
Fetching the rest of the herd around to enjoy them awhile,
Then all uniting to stand on a headland and worry me.

The sentries desert every other part of me,
They have left me helpless to a red marauder,
They all come to the headland to witness and assist against
635   me.

I am given up by traitors;
I talk wildly . . . . I have lost my wits . . . . I and nobody
      else am the greatest traitor,
I went myself first to the headland . . . . my own hands
      carried me there.

You villain touch! what are you doing? . . . . my breath is
      tight in its throat;
640 Unclench your floodgates! you are too much for me.

[29]
Blind loving wrestling touch! Sheathed hooded
    sharptoothed touch!
Did it make you ache so leaving me?

Parting tracked by arriving . . . . perpetual payment of the
    perpetual loan,
Rich showering rain, and recompense richer afterward.

Sprouts take and accumulate . . . . stand by the curb
    prolific and vital,   645
Landscapes projected masculine full-sized and golden.

[30]
All truths wait in all things,
They neither hasten their own delivery nor resist it,
They do not need the obstetric forceps of the surgeon,
The insignificant is as big to me as any,   650
What is less or more than a touch?

Logic and sermons never convince,
The damp of the night drives deeper into my soul.

Only what proves itself to every man and woman is so,
Only what nobody denies is so.   655

A minute and a drop of me settle my brain;
I believe the soggy clods shall become lovers and lamps,
And a compend of compends is the meat of a man or
    woman,
And a summit and flower there is the feeling they have for
    each other,
And they are to branch boundlessly out of that lesson
    until it becomes omnific,   660
And until every one shall delight us, and we them.

[31]
I believe a leaf of grass is no less than the journeywork of
     the stars,
And the pismire is equally perfect, and a grain of sand,
     and the egg of the wren,
And the tree-toad is a chef-d'œuvre for the highest,
And the running blackberry would adorn the parlors of
665   heaven,
And the narrowest hinge in my hand puts to scorn all
     machinery,
And the cow crunching with depressed head surpasses
     any statue,
And a mouse is miracle enough to stagger sextillions of
     infidels,
And I could come every afternoon of my life to look at
     the farmer's girl boiling her iron tea-kettle and baking
     shortcake.

I find I incorporate gneiss and coal and long-threaded
670   moss and fruits and grains and esculent roots,
And am stucco'd with quadrupeds and birds all over,
And have distanced what is behind me for good reasons,
And call any thing close again when I desire it.

In vain the speeding or shyness,
In vain the plutonic rocks send their old heat against my
     approach,
In vain the mastodon retreats beneath its own powdered
675   bones,
In vain objects stand leagues off and assume manifold
     shapes,
In vain the ocean settling in hollows and the great
     monsters lying low,
In vain the buzzard houses herself with the sky,
680 In vain the snake slides through the creepers and logs,
In vain the elk takes to the inner passes of the woods,
In vain the razorbilled auk sails far north to Labrador,

I follow quickly . . . . I ascend to the nest in the fissure of
    the cliff.

[32]

I think I could turn and live awhile with the animals . . . .
    they are so placid and self-contained,
I stand and look at them sometimes half the day long.   685

They do not sweat and whine about their condition,
They do not lie awake in the dark and weep for their sins,
They do not make me sick discussing their duty to God,
Not one is dissatisfied . . . . not one is demented with the
    mania of owning things,
Not one kneels to another nor to his kind that lived
    thousands of years ago,   690
Not one is respectable or industrious over the whole earth.

So they show their relations to me and I accept them;
They bring me tokens of myself . . . . they evince them
    plainly in their possession.

I do not know where they got those tokens,
I must have passed that way untold times ago and
    negligently dropt them,   695
Myself moving forward then and now and forever,
Gathering and showing more always and with velocity,
Infinite and omnigenous and the like of these among
    them;
Not too exclusive toward the reachers of my
    remembrancers,
Picking out here one that shall be my amie,   700
Choosing to go with him on brotherly terms.

A gigantic beauty of a stallion, fresh and responsive to my
    caresses,
Head high in the forehead and wide between the ears,
Limbs glossy and supple, tail dusting the ground,

Eyes well apart and full of sparkling wickedness . . . . ears
705   finely cut and flexibly moving.

His nostrils dilate . . . . my heels embrace him . . . . his
            well built limbs tremble with pleasure . . . . we speed
            around and return.

I but use you a moment and then I resign you stallion . . . .
            and do not need your paces, and outgallop them,
And myself as I stand or sit pass faster than you.

[33]
Swift wind! Space! My Soul! Now I know it is true what I
            guessed at;
710   What I guessed when I loafed on the grass,
        What I guessed while I lay alone in my bed . . . . and again
            as I walked the beach under the paling stars of the
            morning.

My ties and ballasts leave me . . . . I travel . . . . I sail . . . .
            my elbows rest in the sea-gaps,
I skirt the sierras . . . . my palms cover continents,
I am afoot with my vision.

By the city's quadrangular houses . . . . in log-huts, or
715   camping with lumbermen,
        Along the ruts of the turnpike . . . . along the dry gulch
            and rivulet bed,
        Hoeing my onion-patch, and rows of carrots and
            parsnips . . . . crossing savannas . . . . trailing in
            forests,
        Prospecting . . . . gold-digging . . . . girdling the trees of a
            new purchase,
        Scorched ankle-deep by the hot sand . . . . hauling my
            boat down the shallow river;
        Where the panther walks to and fro on a limb
            overhead . . . . where the buck turns furiously at the
720   hunter,

Where the rattlesnake suns his flabby length on a
    rock . . . . where the otter is feeding on fish,
Where the alligator in his tough pimples sleeps by the
    bayou,
Where the black bear is searching for roots or honey . . . .
    where the beaver pats the mud with his paddle-tail;
Over the growing sugar . . . . over the cottonplant . . . .
    over the rice in its low moist field;
Over the sharp-peaked farmhouse with its scalloped scum
    and slender shoots from the gutters;   725
Over the western persimmon . . . . over the longleaved
    corn and the delicate blue-flowered flax;
Over the white and brown buckwheat, a hummer and a
    buzzer there with the rest,
Over the dusky green of the rye as it ripples and shades in
    the breeze;
Scaling mountains . . . . pulling myself cautiously up . . . .
    holding on by low scragged limbs,
Walking the path worn in the grass and beat through the
    leaves of the brush;   730
Where the quail is whistling betwixt the woods and the
    wheatlot,
Where the bat flies in the July eve . . . . where the great
    goldbug drops through the dark;
Where the flails keep time on the barn floor,
Where the brook puts out of the roots of the old tree and
    flows to the meadow,
Where cattle stand and shake away flies with the
    tremulous shuddering of their hides,   735
Where the cheese-cloth hangs in the kitchen, and andirons
    straddle the hearth-slab, and cobwebs fall in festoons
    from the rafters;
Where triphammers crash . . . . where the press is whirling
    its cylinders;
Wherever the human heart beats with terrible throes out
    of its ribs;
Where the pear-shaped balloon is floating aloft . . . .
    floating in it myself and looking composedly down;

Where the life-car is drawn on the slipnoose . . . . where
740   the heat hatches pale-green eggs in the dented sand,
Where the she-whale swims with her calves and never
    forsakes them,
Where the steamship trails hindways its long pennant of
    smoke,
Where the ground-shark's fin cuts like a black chip out of
    the water,
Where the half-burned brig is riding on unknown
    currents,
Where shells grow to her slimy deck, and the dead are
745   corrupting below;
Where the striped and starred flag is borne at the head of
    the regiments;
Approaching Manhattan, up by the long-stretching island,
Under Niagara, the cataract falling like a veil over my
    countenance;
Upon a door-step . . . . upon the horse-block of hard wood
    outside,
Upon the race-course, or enjoying pic-nics or jigs or a
750   good game of base-ball,
At he-festivals with blackguard jibes and ironical license
    and bull-dances and drinking and laughter,
At the cider-mill, tasting the sweet of the brown
    sqush . . . . sucking the juice through a straw,
At apple-peelings, wanting kisses for all the red fruit I
    find,
At musters and beach-parties and friendly bees and
    huskings and house-raisings;
Where the mockingbird sounds his delicious gurgles, and
755   cackles and screams and weeps,
Where the hay-rick stands in the barnyard, and the dry-
    stalks are scattered, and the brood cow waits in the
    hovel,
Where the bull advances to do his masculine work, and
    the stud to the mare, and the cock is treading the hen,
Where the heifers browse, and the geese nip their food
    with short jerks;

Where the sundown shadows lengthen over the limitless
   and lonesome prairie,
Where the herds of buffalo make a crawling spread of the
   square miles far and near;   760
Where the hummingbird shimmers . . . . where the neck of
   the longlived swan is curving and winding;
Where the laughing-gull scoots by the slappy shore and
   laughs her near-human laugh;
Where beehives range on a gray bench in the garden half-
   hid by the high weeds;
Where the band-necked partridges roost in a ring on the
   ground with their heads out;
Where burial coaches enter the arched gates of a cemetery;   765
Where winter wolves bark amid wastes of snow and
   icicled trees;
Where the yellow-crowned heron comes to the edge of the
   marsh at night and feeds upon small crabs;
Where the splash of swimmers and divers cools the warm
   noon;
Where the katydid works her chromatic reed on the
   walnut-tree over the well;
Through patches of citrons and cucumbers with silver-
   wired leaves,   770
Through the salt-lick or orange glade . . . . or under
   conical firs;
Through the gymnasium . . . . through the curtained
   saloon . . . . through the office or public hall;
Pleased with the native and pleased with the foreign . . . .
   pleased with the new and old,
Pleased with women, the homely as well as the
   handsome,
Pleased with the quakeress as she puts off her bonnet and
   talks melodiously,   775
Pleased with the primitive tunes of the choir of the
   whitewashed church,
Pleased with the earnest words of the sweating Methodist
   preacher, or any preacher . . . . looking seriously at the
   camp-meeting;

Looking in at the shop-windows in Broadway the whole
    forenoon . . . . pressing the flesh of my nose to the
    thick plate-glass,
Wandering the same afternoon with my face turned up to
    the clouds;
My right and left arms round the sides of two friends and
780   I in the middle;
Coming home with the bearded and dark-cheeked bush-
    boy . . . . riding behind him at the drape of the day;
Far from the settlements studying the print of animals'
    feet, or the moccasin print;
By the cot in the hospital reaching lemonade to a feverish
    patient,
By the coffined corpse when all is still, examining with a
    candle;
785 Voyaging to every port to dicker and adventure;
Hurrying with the modern crowd, as eager and fickle as any,
Hot toward one I hate, ready in my madness to knife him;
Solitary at midnight in my back yard, my thoughts gone
    from me a long while,
Walking the old hills of Judea with the beautiful gentle
    god by my side;
Speeding through space . . . . speeding through heaven
790   and the stars,
Speeding amid the seven satellites and the broad ring and
    the diameter of eighty thousand miles,
Speeding with tailed meteors . . . . throwing fire-balls like
    the rest,
Carrying the crescent child that carries its own full mother
    in its belly:
Storming enjoying planning loving cautioning,
795 Backing and filling, appearing and disappearing,
I tread day and night such roads.

I visit the orchards of God and look at the spheric product,
And look at quintillions ripened, and look at quintillions
    green.

I fly the flight of the fluid and swallowing soul,
My course runs below the soundings of plummets. 800

I help myself to material and immaterial,
No guard can shut me off, no law can prevent me.

I anchor my ship for a little while only,
My messengers continually cruise away or bring their
     returns to me.

I go hunting polar furs and the seal . . . . leaping chasms
     with a pike-pointed staff . . . . clinging to topples of
     brittle and blue. 805

I ascend to the foretruck . . . . I take my place late at night
     in the crow's nest . . . . we sail through the arctic
     sea . . . . it is plenty light enough,
Through the clear atmosphere I stretch around on the
     wonderful beauty,
The enormous masses of ice pass me and I pass them . . . .
     the scenery is plain in all directions,
The white-topped mountains point up in the distance . . . .
     I fling out my fancies toward them;
We are about approaching some great battlefield in which
     we are soon to be engaged, 810
We pass the colossal outposts of the encampment . . . . we
     pass with still feet and caution;
Or we are entering by the suburbs some vast and ruined
     city . . . . the blocks and fallen architecture more than
     all the living cities of the globe.

I am a free companion . . . . I bivouac by invading
     watchfires.

I turn the bridegroom out of bed and stay with the bride
     myself,
And tighten her all night to my thighs and lips. 815

My voice is the wife's voice, the screech by the rail of the
    stairs,
They fetch my man's body up dripping and drowned.

I understand the large hearts of heroes,
The courage of present times and all times;
How the skipper saw the crowded and rudderless wreck
    of the steamship, and death chasing it up and down
820   the storm,
How he knuckled tight and gave not back one inch, and
    was faithful of days and faithful of nights,
And chalked in large letters on a board, Be of good cheer,
    We will not desert you;
How he saved the drifting company at last,
How the lank loose-gowned women looked when boated
    from the side of their prepared graves,
How the silent old-faced infants, and the lifted sick, and
825   the sharp-lipped unshaved men;
All this I swallow and it tastes good . . . . I like it well, and
    it becomes mine,
I am the man . . . . I suffered . . . . I was there.

The disdain and calmness of martyrs,
The mother condemned for a witch and burnt with dry
    wood, and her children gazing on;
The hounded slave that flags in the race and leans by the
830   fence, blowing and covered with sweat,
The twinges that sting like needles his legs and neck,
The murderous buckshot and the bullets,
All these I feel or am.

I am the hounded slave . . . . I wince at the bite of the dogs,
Hell and despair are upon me . . . . crack and again crack
835   the marksmen,
I clutch the rails of the fence . . . . my gore dribs thinned
    with the ooze of my skin,
I fall on the weeds and stones,
The riders spur their unwilling horses and haul close,

They taunt my dizzy ears . . . . they beat me violently over
   the head with their whip-stocks.

Agonies are one of my changes of garments;   840
I do not ask the wounded person how he feels I
   myself become the wounded person,
My hurt turns livid upon me as I lean on a cane and
   observe.

I am the mashed fireman with breastbone broken . . . .
   tumbling walls buried me in their debris,
Heat and smoke I inspired . . . . I heard the yelling shouts
   of my comrades,
I heard the distant click of their picks and shovels;   845
They have cleared the beams away . . . . they tenderly lift
   me forth.

I lie in the night air in my red shirt . . . . the pervading
   hush is for my sake,
Painless after all I lie, exhausted but not so unhappy,
White and beautiful are the faces around me . . . . the
   heads are bared of their fire-caps,
The kneeling crowd fades with the light of the torches.   850

Distant and dead resuscitate,
They show as the dial or move as the hands of me . . . .
   and I am the clock myself.

I am an old artillerist, and tell of some fort's
   bombardment . . . . and am there again.

Again the reveille of drummers . . . . again the attacking
   cannon and mortars and howitzers,
Again the attacked send their cannon responsive.   855

I take part . . . . I see and hear the whole,
The cries and curses and roar . . . . the plaudits for well
   aimed shots,

The ambulanza slowly passing and trailing its red drip,
Workmen searching after damages and to make
    indispensable repairs,
The fall of grenades through the rent roof . . . . the fan-
    shaped explosion,
The whizz of limbs heads stone wood and iron high in the
860   air.

Again gurgles the mouth of my dying general . . . . he
    furiously waves with his hand,
He gasps through the clot . . . . Mind not me . . . .
    mind . . . . the entrenchments.

[34]
I tell not the fall of Alamo . . . . not one escaped to tell the
    fall of Alamo,
865 The hundred and fifty are dumb yet at Alamo.

Hear now the tale of a jetblack sunrise,
Hear of the murder in cold blood of four hundred and
    twelve young men.

Retreating they had formed in a hollow square with their
    baggage for breastworks,
Nine hundred lives out of the surrounding enemy's nine
    times their number was the price they took in advance,
870 Their colonel was wounded and their ammunition gone,
They treated for an honorable capitulation, received
    writing and seal, gave up their arms, and marched
    back prisoners of war.

They were the glory of the race of rangers,
Matchless with a horse, a rifle, a song, a supper or a
    courtship,
Large, turbulent, brave, handsome, generous, proud and
    affectionate,
875 Bearded, sunburnt, dressed in the free costume of hunters,
Not a single one over thirty years of age.

The second Sunday morning they were brought out in
    squads and massacred . . . . it was beautiful early
    summer,
The work commenced about five o'clock and was over by
    eight.

None obeyed the command to kneel,
Some made a mad and helpless rush . . . . some stood stark
    and straight,   880
A few fell at once, shot in the temple or heart . . . . the
    living and dead lay together,
The maimed and mangled dug in the dirt . . . . the new-
    comers saw them there;
Some half-killed attempted to crawl away,
These were dispatched with bayonets or battered with the
    blunts of muskets;
A youth not seventeen years old seized his assassin till two
    more came to release him,   885
The three were all torn, and covered with the boy's blood.

At eleven o'clock began the burning of the bodies;
And that is the tale of the murder of the four hundred and
    twelve young men,
And that was a jetblack sunrise.

[35]
Did you read in the seabooks of the oldfashioned frigate-
    fight?   890
Did you learn who won by the light of the moon and stars?

Our foe was no skulk in his ship, I tell you,
His was the English pluck, and there is no tougher or
    truer, and never was, and never will be;
Along the lowered eve he came, horribly raking us.

We closed with him . . . . the yards entangled . . . . the
    cannon touched,   895
My captain lashed fast with his own hands.

We had received some eighteen-pound shots under the
    water,
On our lower-gun-deck two large pieces had burst at the
    first fire, killing all around and blowing up overhead.

Ten o'clock at night, and the full moon shining and the
    leaks on the gain, and five feet of water reported,
The master-at-arms loosing the prisoners confined in the
900   after-hold to give them a chance for themselves.

The transit to and from the magazine was now stopped by
    the sentinels,
They saw so many strange faces they did not know whom
    to trust.

Our frigate was afire . . . . the other asked if we demanded
    quarters? if our colors were struck and the fighting
    done?

I laughed content when I heard the voice of my little
    captain,
We have not struck, he composedly cried, We have just
905   begun our part of the fighting.

Only three guns were in use,
One was directed by the captain himself against the
    enemy's mainmast,
Two well-served with grape and canister silenced his
    musketry and cleared his decks.

The tops alone seconded the fire of this little battery,
    especially the maintop,
910 They all held out bravely during the whole of the action.

Not a moment's cease,
The leaks gained fast on the pumps . . . . the fire eat toward
    the powder-magazine,

One of the pumps was shot away . . . . it was generally
    thought we were sinking.

Serene stood the little captain,
He was not hurried . . . . his voice was neither high nor
    low,   915
His eyes gave more light to us than our battle-lanterns.

Toward twelve at night, there in the beams of the moon
    they surrendered to us.

[36]

Stretched and still lay the midnight,
Two great hulls motionless on the breast of the
    darkness,
Our vessel riddled and slowly sinking . . . . preparations
    to pass to the one we had conquered,   920
The captain on the quarter deck coldly giving his orders
    through a countenance white as a sheet,
Near by the corpse of the child that served in the cabin,
The dead face of an old salt with long white hair and
    carefully curled whiskers,
The flames spite of all that could be done flickering aloft
    and below,
The husky voices of the two or three officers yet fit for
    duty,   925
Formless stacks of bodies and bodies by themselves . . . .
    dabs of flesh upon the masts and spars,
The cut of cordage and dangle of rigging . . . . the slight
    shock of the soothe of waves,
Black and impassive guns, and litter of powder-parcels,
    and the strong scent,
Delicate sniffs of the seabreeze . . . . smells of sedgy grass
    and fields by the shore . . . . death-messages given in
    charge to survivors,
The hiss of the surgeon's knife and the gnawing teeth of
    his saw,   930

The wheeze, the cluck, the swash of falling blood . . . . the
    short wild scream, the long dull tapering groan,
These so . . . . these irretrievable.

[37]
O Christ! My fit is mastering me!
What the rebel said gaily adjusting his throat to the rope-
    noose,
What the savage at the stump, his eye-sockets empty, his
935   mouth spirting whoops and defiance,
What stills the traveler come to the vault at Mount
    Vernon,
What sobers the Brooklyn boy as he looks down the shores
    of the Wallabout and remembers the prison ships,
What burnt the gums of the redcoat at Saratoga when he
    surrendered his brigades,
These become mine and me every one, and they are but
    little,
940 I become as much more as I like.

I become any presence or truth of humanity here,
And see myself in prison shaped like another man,
And feel the dull unintermitted pain.

For me the keepers of convicts shoulder their carbines and
    keep watch,
945 It is I let out in the morning and barred at night.

Not a mutineer walks handcuffed to the jail, but I am
    handcuffed to him and walk by his side,
I am less the jolly one there, and more the silent one with
    sweat on my twitching lips.

Not a youngster is taken for larceny, but I go too and am
    tried and sentenced.

Not a cholera patient lies at the last gasp, but I also lie at
    the last gasp,

My face is ash-colored, my sinews gnarl . . . . away from
    me people retreat.   950

Askers embody themselves in me, and I am embodied in
    them,
I project my hat and sit shamefaced and beg.

I rise extatic through all, and sweep with the true
    gravitation,
The whirling and whirling is elemental within me.

[38]
Somehow I have been stunned. Stand back!   955
Give me a little time beyond my cuffed head and slumbers
    and dreams and gaping,
I discover myself on a verge of the usual mistake.

That I could forget the mockers and insults!
That I could forget the trickling tears and the blows of the
    bludgeons and hammers!
That I could look with a separate look on my own
    crucifixion and bloody crowning!   960

I remember . . . . I resume the overstaid fraction,
The grave of rock multiplies what has been confided to
    it . . . . or to any graves,
The corpses rise . . . . the gashes heal . . . . the fastenings
    roll away.

I troop forth replenished with supreme power, one of an
    average unending procession,
We walk the roads of Ohio and Massachusetts and
    Virginia and Wisconsin and New York and New
    Orleans and Texas and Montreal and San Francisco
    and Charleston and Savannah and Mexico,   965
Inland and by the seacoast and boundary lines . . . . and
    we pass the boundary lines.

Our swift ordinances are on their way over the whole
    earth,
The blossoms we wear in our hats are the growth of two
    thousand years.

Eleves I salute you,
I see the approach of your numberless gangs . . . . I see you
970   understand yourselves and me,
And know that they who have eyes are divine, and the
    blind and lame are equally divine,
And that my steps drag behind yours yet go before them,
And are aware how I am with you no more than I am
    with everybody.

[39]
The friendly and flowing savage . . . . Who is he?
975 Is he waiting for civilization or past it and mastering it?

Is he some southwesterner raised outdoors? Is he Canadian?
Is he from the Mississippi country? or from Iowa, Oregon
    or California? or from the mountain? or prairie life or
    bush-life? or from the sea?

Wherever he goes men and women accept and desire him,
They desire he should like them and touch them and speak
    to them and stay with them.

Behaviour lawless as snow-flakes . . . . words simple as
980   grass . . . . uncombed head and laughter and naivete;
Slowstepping feet and the common features, and the
    common modes and emanations,
They descend in new forms from the tips of his fingers,
They are wafted with the odor of his body or breath . . . .
    they fly out of the glance of his eyes.

[40]
Flaunt of the sunshine I need not your bask . . . . lie over,
You light surfaces only . . . . I force the surfaces and the
985   depths also.

Earth! you seem to look for something at my hands,
Say old topknot! what do you want?

Man or woman! I might tell how I like you, but cannot,
And might tell what it is in me and what it is in you, but
    cannot,
And might tell the pinings I have . . . . the pulse of my
    nights and days.   990

Behold I do not give lectures or a little charity,
What I give I give out of myself.

You there, impotent, loose in the knees, open your scarfed
    chops till I blow grit within you,
Spread your palms and lift the flaps of your pockets,
I am not to be denied . . . . I compel . . . . I have stores
    plenty and to spare,   995
And any thing I have I bestow.

I do not ask who you are . . . . that is not important to me,
You can do nothing and be nothing but what I will infold
    you.

To a drudge of the cottonfields or emptier of privies I
    lean . . . . on his right cheek I put the family kiss,
And in my soul I swear I never will deny him.   1000

On women fit for conception I start bigger and nimbler
    babes,
This day I am jetting the stuff of far more arrogant
    republics.

To any one dying . . . . thither I speed and twist the knob
    of the door,
Turn the bedclothes toward the foot of the bed,
Let the physician and the priest go home.   1005

I seize the descending man . . . . I raise him with resistless
    will.

O despairer, here is my neck,
By God! you shall not go down! Hang your whole
    weight upon me.

I dilate you with tremendous breath . . . . I buoy you up;
Every room of the house do I fill with an armed
1010   force . . . . lovers of me, bafflers of graves:
Sleep! I and they keep guard all night;
Not doubt, not decease shall dare to lay finger upon
    you,
I have embraced you, and henceforth possess you to
    myself,
And when you rise in the morning you will find what I tell
    you is so.

[41]
I am he bringing help for the sick as they pant on their
1015   backs,
And for strong upright men I bring yet more needed help.

I heard what was said of the universe,
Heard it and heard of several thousand years;
It is middling well as far as it goes . . . . but is that all?

1020 Magnifying and applying come I,
    Outbidding at the start the old cautious hucksters,
    The most they offer for mankind and eternity less than a
        spirt of my own seminal wet,
    Taking myself the exact dimensions of Jehovah and
        laying them away,
    Lithographing Kronos and Zeus his son, and Hercules
        his grandson,
    Buying drafts of Osiris and Isis and Belus and Brahma
1025   and Adonai,
    In my portfolio placing Manito loose, and Allah on a
        leaf, and the crucifix engraved,
    With Odin, and the hideous-faced Mexitli, and all idols
        and images,

Honestly taking them all for what they are worth, and
    not a cent more,
Admitting they were alive and did the work of their
    day,
Admitting they bore mites as for unfledged birds who
    have now to rise and fly and sing for themselves,   1030
Accepting the rough deific sketches to fill out better in
    myself . . . . bestowing them freely on each man and
    woman I see,
Discovering as much or more in a framer framing a
    house,
Putting higher claims for him there with his rolled-up
    sleeves, driving the mallet and chisel;
Not objecting to special revelations . . . . considering a
    curl of smoke or a hair on the back of my hand as
    curious as any revelation;
Those ahold of fire-engines and hook-and-ladder ropes
    more to me than the gods of the antique wars,   1035
Minding their voices peal through the crash of
    destruction,
Their brawny limbs passing safe over charred laths . . . .
    their white foreheads whole and unhurt out of the
    flames;
By the mechanic's wife with her babe at her nipple
    interceding for every person born;
Three scythes at harvest whizzing in a row from three
    lusty angels with shirts bagged out at their waists;
The snag-toothed hostler with red hair redeeming sins
    past and to come,   1040
Selling all he possesses and traveling on foot to fee
    lawyers for his brother and sit by him while he is
    tried for forgery:
What was strewn in the amplest strewing the square rod
    about me, and not filling the square rod then;
The bull and the bug never worshipped half enough,
Dung and dirt more admirable than was dreamed,
The supernatural of no account . . . . myself waiting my
    time to be one of the supremes,   1045

The day getting ready for me when I shall do as much
    good as the best, and be as prodigious,
Guessing when I am it will not tickle me much to receive
    puffs out of pulpit or print;
By my life-lumps! becoming already a creator!
Putting myself here and now to the ambushed womb of
    the shadows!

[42]

1050 .... A call in the midst of the crowd,
My own voice, orotund sweeping and final.

Come my children,
Come my boys and girls, and my women and household
    and intimates,
Now the performer launches his nerve .... he has passed
    his prelude on the reeds within.

Easily written loosefingered chords! I feel the thrum of
1055   their climax and close.

My head evolves on my neck,
Music rolls, but not from the organ .... folks are around
    me, but they are no household of mine.

Ever the hard and unsunk ground,
Ever the eaters and drinkers .... ever the upward and
    downward sun .... ever the air and the ceaseless
    tides,
Ever myself and my neighbors, refreshing and wicked
1060   and real,
Ever the old inexplicable query .... ever that thorned
    thumb—that breath of itches and thirsts,
Ever the vexer's hoot! hoot! till we find where the sly
    one hides and bring him forth;
Ever love .... ever the sobbing liquid of life,
Ever the bandage under the chin .... ever the trestles of
    death.

Here and there with dimes on the eyes walking,   1065
To feed the greed of the belly the brains liberally
    spooning,
Tickets buying or taking or selling, but in to the feast
    never once going;
Many sweating and ploughing and thrashing, and then
    the chaff for payment receiving,
A few idly owning, and they the wheat continually
    claiming.

This is the city . . . . and I am one of the citizens;   1070
Whatever interests the rest interests me . . . . politics,
    churches, newspapers, schools,
Benevolent societies, improvements, banks, tariffs,
    steamships, factories, markets,
Stocks and stores and real estate and personal estate.

They who piddle and patter here in collars and tailed
    coats . . . . I am aware who they are . . . . and that
    they are not worms or fleas,
I acknowledge the duplicates of myself under all the
    scrape-lipped and pipe-legged concealments.   1075

The weakest and shallowest is deathless with me,
What I do and say the same waits for them,
Every thought that flounders in me the same flounders in
    them.

I know perfectly well my own egotism,
And know my omnivorous words, and cannot say any
    less,   1080
And would fetch you whoever you are flush with
    myself.

My words are words of a questioning, and to indicate
    reality;
This printed and bound book . . . . but the printer and the
    printing-office boy?

The marriage estate and settlement . . . . but the body and
    mind of the bridegroom? also those of the bride?
1085 The panorama of the sea . . . . but the sea itself?
The well-taken photographs . . . . but your wife or friend
    close and solid in your arms?
The fleet of ships of the line and all the modern
    improvements . . . . but the craft and pluck of the
    admiral?
The dishes and fare and furniture . . . . but the host and
    hostess, and the look out of their eyes?
The sky up there . . . . yet here or next door or across the
    way?
1090 The saints and sages in history . . . . but you yourself?
Sermons and creeds and theology . . . . but the human
    brain, and what is called reason, and what is called
    love, and what is called life?

[43]
I do not despise you priests;
My faith is the greatest of faiths and the least of faiths,
Enclosing all worship ancient and modern, and all
    between ancient and modern,
Believing I shall come again upon the earth after five
1095   thousand years,
Waiting responses from oracles . . . . honoring the
    gods . . . . saluting the sun,
Making a fetish of the first rock or stump . . . . powowing
    with sticks in the circle of obis,
Helping the lama or brahmin as he trims the lamps of
    the idols,
Dancing yet through the streets in a phallic
    procession . . . . rapt and austere in the woods, a
    gymnosophist,
Drinking mead from the skull-cup . . . . to shasta and
1100   vedas admirant . . . . minding the koran,
Walking the teokallis, spotted with gore from the stone
    and knife—beating the serpent-skin drum;

Accepting the gospels, accepting him that was crucified,
    knowing assuredly that he is divine,
To the mass kneeling—to the puritan's prayer rising—
    sitting patiently in a pew,
Ranting and frothing in my insane crisis—waiting dead-
    like till my spirit arouses me;
Looking forth on pavement and land, and outside of
    pavement and land,   1105
Belonging to the winders of the circuit of circuits.

One of that centripetal and centrifugal gang,
I turn and talk like a man leaving charges before a journey.

Down-hearted doubters, dull and excluded,
Frivolous sullen moping angry affected disheartened
    atheistical,
I know every one of you, and know the unspoken
    interrogatories,   1110
By experience I know them.

How the flukes splash!
How they contort rapid as lightning, with spasms and
    spouts of blood!

Be at peace bloody flukes of doubters and sullen mopers,   1115
I take my place among you as much as among any;
The past is the push of you and me and all precisely the
    same,
And the day and night are for you and me and all,
And what is yet untried and afterward is for you and me
    and all.

I do not know what is untried and afterward,   1120
But I know it is sure and alive and sufficient.

Each who passes is considered, and each who stops is
    considered, and not a single one can it fail.

It cannot fail the young man who died and was buried,
Nor the young woman who died and was put by his side,
Nor the little child that peeped in at the door and then
1125   drew back and was never seen again,
Nor the old man who has lived without purpose, and
          feels it with bitterness worse than gall,
Nor him in the poorhouse tubercled by rum and the bad
          disorder,
Nor the numberless slaughtered and wrecked . . . . nor
          the brutish koboo, called the ordure of humanity,
Nor the sacs merely floating with open mouths for food
          to slip in,
Nor any thing in the earth, or down in the oldest graves
1130   of the earth,
Nor any thing in the myriads of spheres, nor one of the
          myriads of myriads that inhabit them,
Nor the present, nor the least wisp that is known.

                         [44]
It is time to explain myself . . . . let us stand up.

What is known I strip away . . . . I launch all men and
          women forward with me into the unknown.

The clock indicates the moment . . . . but what does
1135   eternity indicate?
Eternity lies in bottomless reservoirs . . . . its buckets are
          rising forever and ever,
They pour and they pour and they exhale away.

We have thus far exhausted trillions of winters and
          summers;
There are trillions ahead, and trillions ahead of them.

Births have brought us richness and variety,
1140 And other births will bring us richness and variety.

I do not call one greater and one smaller,
That which fills its period and place is equal to any.

Were mankind murderous or jealous upon you my
    brother or my sister?
I am sorry for you . . . . they are not murderous or jealous
    upon me;   1145
All has been gentle with me . . . . I keep no account with
    lamentation;
What have I to do with lamentation?

I am an acme of things accomplished, and I an encloser
    of things to be.

My feet strike an apex of the apices of the stairs,
On every step bunches of ages, and larger bunches
    between the steps,   1150
All below duly traveled—and still I mount and mount.

Rise after rise bow the phantoms behind me,
Afar down I see the huge first Nothing, the vapor from
    the nostrils of death,
I know I was even there . . . . I waited unseen and always,
And slept while God carried me through the lethargic
    mist,   1155
And took my time . . . . and took no hurt from the fœtid
    carbon.

Long I was hugged close . . . . long and long.

Immense have been the preparations for me,
Faithful and friendly the arms that have helped me.

Cycles ferried my cradle, rowing and rowing like cheerful
    boatmen;   1160
For room to me stars kept aside in their own rings,
They sent influences to look after what was to hold me.

Before I was born out of my mother generations guided me,
My embryo has never been torpid . . . . nothing could
    overlay it;

For it the nebula cohered to an orb . . . . the long slow
    strata piled to rest it on . . . . vast vegetables gave it
1165   sustenance,
Monstrous sauroids transported it in their mouths and
    deposited it with care.

All forces have been steadily employed to complete and
    delight me,
Now I stand on this spot with my soul.

[45]
Span of youth! Ever-pushed elasticity! Manhood balanced
    and florid and full!

1170 My lovers suffocate me!
Crowding my lips, and thick in the pores of my skin,
Jostling me through streets and public halls . . . . coming
    naked to me at night,
Crying by day Ahoy from the rocks of the river . . . .
    swinging and chirping over my head,
Calling my name from flowerbeds or vines or tangled
    underbrush,
Or while I swim in the bath . . . . or drink from the
    pump at the corner . . . . or the curtain is down at the
    opera . . . . or I glimpse at a woman's face in the
1175   railroad car;
Lighting on every moment of my life,
Bussing my body with soft and balsamic busses,
Noiselessly passing handfuls out of their hearts and
    giving them to be mine.

Old age superbly rising! Ineffable grace of dying days!
Every condition promulges not only itself . . . . it
1180   promulges what grows after and out of itself,
And the dark hush promulges as much as any.

I open my scuttle at night and see the far-sprinkled systems,
And all I see, multiplied as high as I can cipher, edge but
    the rim of the farther systems.

Wider and wider they spread, expanding and always
    expanding,
Outward and outward and forever outward.   1185

My sun has his sun, and round him obediently wheels,
He joins with his partners a group of superior circuit,
And greater sets follow, making specks of the greatest
    inside them.

There is no stoppage, and never can be stoppage;
If I and you and the worlds and all beneath or upon their
    surfaces, and all the palpable life, were this moment
    reduced back to a pallid float, it would not avail in
    the long run,   1190
We should surely bring up again where we now stand,
And as surely go as much farther, and then farther and
    farther.

A few quadrillions of eras, a few octillions of cubic
    leagues, do not hazard the span, or make it impatient,
They are but parts . . . . any thing is but a part.

See ever so far . . . . there is limitless space outside of that, 1195
Count ever so much . . . . there is limitless time around that.

Our rendezvous is fitly appointed . . . . God will be there
    and wait till we come.

[46]
I know I have the best of time and space—and that I was
    never measured, and never will be measured.

I tramp a perpetual journey,
My signs are a rain-proof coat and good shoes and a
    staff cut from the woods;   1200
No friend of mine takes his ease in my chair,
I have no chair, nor church nor philosophy;
I lead no man to a dinner-table or library or exchange,

But each man and each woman of you I lead upon a knoll,
1205 My left hand hooks you round the waist,
My right hand points to landscapes of continents, and a
    plain public road.

Not I, not any one else can travel that road for you,
You must travel it for yourself.

It is not far . . . . it is within reach,
Perhaps you have been on it since you were born, and
1210   did not know,
Perhaps it is every where on water and on land.

Shoulder your duds, and I will mine, and let us hasten
    forth;
Wonderful cities and free nations we shall fetch as we go.

If you tire, give me both burdens, and rest the chuff of
    your hand on my hip,
1215 And in due time you shall repay the same service to me;
For after we start we never lie by again.

This day before dawn I ascended a hill and looked at the
    crowded heaven,
And I said to my spirit, When we become the enfolders
    of those orbs and the pleasure and knowledge of
    every thing in them, shall we be filled and satisfied
    then?
And my spirit said No, we level that lift to pass and
    continue beyond.

1220 You are also asking me questions, and I hear you;
I answer that I cannot answer . . . . you must find out for
    yourself.

Sit awhile wayfarer,
Here are biscuits to eat and here is milk to drink,

But as soon as you sleep and renew yourself in sweet
    clothes I will certainly kiss you with my goodbye
    kiss and open the gate for your egress hence.

Long enough have you dreamed contemptible dreams,   1225
Now I wash the gum from your eyes,
You must habit yourself to the dazzle of the light and
    of every moment of your life.

Long have you timidly waded, holding a plank by the
    shore,
Now I will you to be a bold swimmer,
To jump off in the midst of the sea, and rise again and
    nod to me and shout, and laughingly dash with your
    hair.   1230

[47]

I am the teacher of athletes,
He that by me spreads a wider breast than my own
    proves the width of my own,
He most honors my style who learns under it to destroy
    the teacher.

The boy I love, the same becomes a man not through
    derived power but in his own right,
Wicked, rather than virtuous out of conformity or fear,   1235
Fond of his sweetheart, relishing well his steak,
Unrequited love or a slight cutting him worse than a
    wound cuts,
First rate to ride, to fight, to hit the bull's eye, to sail a
    skiff, to sing a song or play on the banjo,
Preferring scars and faces pitted with smallpox over all
    latherers and those that keep out of the sun.

I teach straying from me, yet who can stray from me?   1240
I follow you whoever you are from the present hour;
My words itch at your ears till you understand them.

I do not say these things for a dollar, or to fill up the
 time while I wait for a boat;
It is you talking just as much as myself . . . . I act as the
 tongue of you,
It was tied in your mouth . . . . in mine it begins to be
1245   loosened.

I swear I will never mention love or death inside a house,
And I swear I never will translate myself at all, only to him
 or her who privately stays with me in the open air.

If you would understand me go to the heights or water-
 shore,
The nearest gnat is an explanation and a drop or the
 motion of waves a key,
1250 The maul the oar and the handsaw second my words.

No shuttered room or school can commune with me,
But roughs and little children better than they.

The young mechanic is closest to me . . . . he knows me
 pretty well,
The woodman that takes his axe and jug with him shall
 take me with him all day,
The farmboy ploughing in the field feels good at the
1255   sound of my voice,
In vessels that sail my words must sail . . . . I go with
 fishermen and seamen, and love them,
My face rubs to the hunter's face when he lies down
 alone in his blanket,
The driver thinking of me does not mind the jolt of his
 wagon,
The young mother and old mother shall comprehend me,
The girl and the wife rest the needle a moment and
1260   forget where they are,
They and all would resume what I have told them.

[48]

I have said that the soul is not more than the body,
And I have said that the body is not more than the soul,
And nothing, not God, is greater to one than one's-self is,
And whoever walks a furlong without sympathy walks to
    his own funeral, dressed in his shroud,   1265
And I or you pocketless of a dime may purchase the pick
    of the earth,
And to glance with an eye or show a bean in its pod
    confounds the learning of all times,
And there is no trade or employment but the young man
    following it may become a hero,
And there is no object so soft but it makes a hub for the
    wheeled universe,
And any man or woman shall stand cool and supercilious
    before a million universes.   1270

And I call to mankind, Be not curious about God,
For I who am curious about each am not curious about
    God,
No array of terms can say how much I am at peace about
    God and about death.

I hear and behold God in every object, yet I understand
    God not in the least,
Nor do I understand who there can be more wonderful
    than myself.   1275

Why should I wish to see God better than this day?
I see something of God each hour of the twenty-four, and
    each moment then,
In the faces of men and women I see God, and in my own
    face in the glass;
I find letters from God dropped in the street, and every
    one is signed by God's name,
And I leave them where they are, for I know that others
    will punctually come forever and ever.   1280

[49]
And as to you death, and you bitter hug of mortality . . . .
    it is idle to try to alarm me.

To his work without flinching the accoucheur comes,
I see the elderhand pressing receiving supporting,
I recline by the sills of the exquisite flexible doors . . . .
    and mark the outlet, and mark the relief and escape.

And as to you corpse I think you are good manure, but
1285   that does not offend me,
I smell the white roses sweetscented and growing,
I reach to the leafy lips . . . . I reach to the polished
    breasts of melons,

And as to you life, I reckon you are the leavings of many
    deaths,
No doubt I have died myself ten thousand times before.

1290 I hear you whispering there O stars of heaven,
O suns . . . . O grass of graves . . . . O perpetual transfers
    and promotions . . . . if you do not say anything how
    can I say anything?

Of the turbid pool that lies in the autumn forest,
Of the moon that descends the steeps of the soughing
    twilight,
Toss, sparkles of day and dusk . . . . toss on the black
    stems that decay in the muck,
1295 Toss to the moaning gibberish of the dry limbs.

I ascend from the moon . . . . I ascend from the night,
And perceive of the ghastly glitter the sunbeams reflected,
And debouch to the steady and central from the
    offspring great or small.

[50]

There is that in me . . . . I do not know what it is . . . . but
    I know it is in me.
Wrenched and sweaty . . . . calm and cool then my body
    becomes;   1300
I sleep . . . . I sleep long.

I do not know it . . . . it is without name . . . . it is a word
    unsaid,
It is not in any dictionary or utterance or symbol.

Something it swings on more than the earth I swing
    on,
To it the creation is the friend whose embracing awakes
    me.   1305

Perhaps I might tell more . . . . Outlines! I plead for my
    brothers and sisters.

Do you see O my brothers and sisters?
It is not chaos or death . . . . it is form and union and
    plan . . . . it is eternal life . . . . it is happiness.

[51]

The past and present wilt . . . . I have filled them and
    emptied them,
And proceed to fill my next fold of the future.   1310

Listener up there! Here you . . . . what have you to
    confide to me?
Look in my face while I snuff the sidle of evening,
Talk honestly, for no one else hears you, and I stay only
    a minute longer.

Do I contradict myself?
Very well then . . . . I contradict myself;   1315
I am large . . . . I contain multitudes.

I concentrate toward them that are nigh . . . . I wait on
    the door-slab.

Who has done his day's work and will soonest be through
    with his supper?
Who wishes to walk with me?

Will you speak before I am gone? Will you prove already
1320   too late?

[52]
The spotted hawk swoops by and accuses me . . . . he
    complains of my gab and my loitering.

I too am not a bit tamed . . . . I too am untranslatable,
I sound my barbaric yawp over the roofs of the world.

The last scud of day holds back for me,
It flings my likeness after the rest and true as any on the
1325   shadowed wilds,
It coaxes me to the vapor and the dusk.

I depart as air . . . . I shake my white locks at the runaway
    sun,
I effuse my flesh in eddies and drift it in lacy jags.

I bequeath myself to the dirt to grow from the grass I
    love,
1330 If you want me again look for me under your bootsoles.

You will hardly know who I am or what I mean,
But I shall be good health to you nevertheless,
And filter and fibre your blood.

Failing to fetch me at first keep encouraged,
1335 Missing me one place search another,
I stop some where waiting for you

LEAVES OF GRASS

[A Song for Occupations]

[1]

Come closer to me,
Push close my lovers and take the best I possess,
Yield closer and closer and give me the best you
    possess.

This is unfinished business with me . . . . how is it with
    you?
I was chilled with the cold types and cylinder and wet
    paper between us.   5

I pass so poorly with paper and types . . . . I must pass
    with the contact of bodies and souls.

I do not thank you for liking me as I am, and liking the
    touch of me . . . . I know that it is good for you to
    do so.

Were all educations practical and ornamental well
    displayed out of me, what would it amount to?
Were I as the head teacher or charitable proprietor or wise
    statesman, what would it amount to?
Were I to you as the boss employing and paying you,
    would that satisfy you?   10

The learned and virtuous and benevolent, and the usual
    terms;
A man like me, and never the usual terms.

Neither a servant nor a master am I,
I take no sooner a large price than a small price . . . . I will
    have my own whoever enjoys me,
15 I will be even with you, and you shall be even with me.

If you are a workman or workwoman I stand as nigh as
    the nighest that works in the same shop,
If you bestow gifts on your brother or dearest friend,
    I demand as good as your brother or dearest
    friend,
If your lover or husband or wife is welcome by day or
    night, I must be personally as welcome;
If you have become degraded or ill, then I will become so
    for your sake;
If you remember your foolish and outlawed deeds, do you
    think I cannot remember my foolish and outlawed
20   deeds?
If you carouse at the table I say I will carouse at the
    opposite side of the table;
If you meet some stranger in the street and love him or
    her, do I not often meet strangers in the street and
    love them?
If you see a good deal remarkable in me I see just as much
    remarkable in you.

Why what have you thought of yourself?
25 Is it you then that thought yourself less?
Is it you that thought the President greater than you? or
    the rich better off than you? or the educated wiser
    than you?

Because you are greasy or pimpled—or that you was once
    drunk, or a thief, or diseased, or rheumatic, or a
    prostitute—or are so now—or from frivolity or
    impotence—or that you are no scholar, and never saw
    your name in print . . . . do you give in that you are
    any less immortal?

[2]

Souls of men and women! it is not you I call unseen,
  unheard, untouchable and untouching;
It is not you I go argue pro and con about, and to settle
  whether you are alive or no;
I own publicly who you are, if nobody else owns . . . . and
  see and hear you, and what you give and take;   30
What is there you cannot give and take?

I see not merely that you are polite or whitefaced . . . .
  married or single . . . . citizens of old states or citizens
  of new states . . . . eminent in some profession . . . . a
  lady or gentleman in a parlor . . . . or dressed in the jail
  uniform . . . . or pulpit uniform,
Not only the free Utahan, Kansian, or Arkansian . . . . not
  only the free Cuban . . . not merely the slave . . . .
  not Mexican native, or Flatfoot, or negro from
  Africa,
Iroquois eating the warflesh—fishtearer in his lair of rocks
  and sand . . . . Esquimaux in the dark cold
  snowhouse . . . . Chinese with his transverse eyes. . . .
  Bedowee—or wandering nomad—or tabounschik at
  the head of his droves,
Grown, half-grown, and babe—of this country and every
  country, indoors and outdoors I see . . . . and all else is
  behind or through them.   35

The wife—and she is not one jot less than the husband,
The daughter—and she is just as good as the son,
The mother—and she is every bit as much as the father.

Offspring of those not rich—boys apprenticed to trades,
Young fellows working on farms and old fellows working
  on farms;   40
The naive . . . . the simple and hardy . . . . he going to the
  polls to vote . . . . he who has a good time, and he
  who has a bad time;

Mechanics, southerners, new arrivals, sailors,
   mano'warsmen, merchantmen, coasters,
   All these I see . . . . but nigher and farther the same I see;
   None shall escape me, and none shall wish to escape me.

45 I bring what you much need, yet always have,
   I bring not money or amours or dress or eating . . . . but I
     bring as good;
   And send no agent or medium . . . . and offer no
     representative of value—but offer the value itself.

There is something that comes home to one now and
    perpetually,
   It is not what is printed or preached or discussed . . . . it
     eludes discussion and print,
50 It is not to be put in a book . . . . it is not in this book,
   It is for you whoever you are . . . . it is no farther from you
     than your hearing and sight are from you,
   It is hinted by nearest and commonest and readiest . . . . it
     is not them, though it is endlessly provoked by
     them . . . . What is there ready and near you now?

You may read in many languages and read nothing about
    it;
   You may read the President's message and read nothing
     about it there;
   Nothing in the reports from the state department or
     treasury department . . . . or in the daily papers, or the
55   weekly papers,
   Or in the census returns or assessors' returns or prices
     current or any accounts of stock.

[3]
The sun and stars that float in the open air . . . . the
    appleshaped earth and we upon it . . . . surely the drift
    of them is something grand;
   I do not know what it is except that it is grand, and that it
    is happiness,

And that the enclosing purport of us here is not a
    speculation, or bon-mot or reconnoissance,
And that it is not something which by luck may turn out
    well for us, and without luck must be a failure for us,   60
And not something which may yet be retracted in a
    certain contingency.

The light and shade—the curious sense of body and
    identity—the greed that with perfect complaisance
    devours all things—the endless pride and
    outstretching of man—unspeakable joys and
    sorrows,
The wonder every one sees in every one else he sees . . . .
    and the wonders that fill each minute of time forever
    and each acre of surface and space forever,
Have you reckoned them as mainly for a trade or
    farmwork? or for the profits of a store? or to achieve
    yourself a position? or to fill a gentleman's leisure or
    a lady's leisure?

Have you reckoned the landscape took substance and
    form that it might be painted in a picture?   65
Or men and women that they might be written of, and
    songs sung?
Or the attraction of gravity and the great laws and
    harmonious combinations and the fluids of the air as
    subjects for the savans?
Or the brown land and the blue sea for maps and charts?
Or the stars to be put in constellations and named fancy
    names?
Or that the growth of seeds is for agricultural tables or
    agriculture itself?   70

Old institutions . . . . these arts libraries legends
    collections—and the practice handed along in
    manufactures . . . . will we rate them so high?
Will we rate our prudence and business so high? I
    have no objection,

I rate them as high as the highest . . . . but a child born of
a woman and man I rate beyond all rate.

We thought our Union grand and our Constitution
grand;
75 I do not say they are not grand and good—for they are,
I am this day just as much in love with them as you,
But I am eternally in love with you and with all my
fellows upon the earth.

We consider the bibles and religions divine . . . . I do not
say they are not divine,
I say they have all grown out of you and may grow out of
you still,
It is not they who give the life . . . . it is you who give the
80 life;
Leaves are not more shed from the trees or trees from the
earth than they are shed out of you.

[4]
The sum of all known value and respect I add up in you
whoever you are;
The President is up there in the White House for you . . . .
it is not you who are here for him,
The Secretaries act in their bureaus for you . . . . not you
here for them,
85 The Congress convenes every December for you,
Laws, courts, the forming of states, the charters of cities,
the going and coming of commerce and mails are all
for you.

All doctrines, all politics and civilization exurge from
you,
All sculpture and monuments and anything inscribed
anywhere are tallied in you,
The gist of histories and statistics as far back as the
records reach is in you this hour—and myths and tales
the same;

If you were not breathing and walking here where would
    they all be?   90
The most renowned poems would be ashes . . . . orations
    and plays would be vacuums.

All architecture is what you do to it when you look upon
    it;
Did you think it was in the white or gray stone? or the
    lines of the arches and cornices?

All music is what awakens from you when you are
    reminded by the instruments,
It is not the violins and the cornets . . . . it is not the oboe
    nor the beating drums—nor the notes of the baritone
    singer singing his sweet romanza . . . . nor those of the
    men's chorus, nor those of the women's chorus,   95
It is nearer and farther than they.

[5]
Will the whole come back then?
Can each see the signs of the best by a look in the
    lookingglass? Is there nothing greater or more?
Does all sit there with you and here with me?

The old forever new things . . . . you foolish child! . . . . the
    closest simplest things—this moment with you,   100
Your person and every particle that relates to your person,
The pulses of your brain waiting their chance and
    encouragement at every deed or sight;
Anything you do in public by day, and anything you do in
    secret betweendays,
What is called right and what is called wrong . . . . what
    you behold or touch . . . . what causes your anger or
    wonder,
The anklechain of the slave, the bed of the bedhouse, the
    cards of the gambler, the plates of the forger;   105
What is seen or learned in the street, or intuitively
    learned,

What is learned in the public school—spelling, reading,
    writing and ciphering . . . . the blackboard and the
    teacher's diagrams:
The panes of the windows and all that appears through
    them . . . . the going forth in the morning and the
    aimless spending of the day;
(What is it that you made money? what is it that you got
    what you wanted?)
The usual routine . . . . the workshop, factory, yard,
110   office, store, or desk;
The jaunt of hunting or fishing, or the life of hunting or
    fishing,
Pasturelife, foddering, milking and herding, and all the
    personnel and usages;
The plum-orchard and apple-orchard . . . . gardening . . . .
    seedlings, cuttings, flowers and vines,
Grains and manures . . marl, clay, loam . . the subsoil
    plough . . the shovel and pick and rake and hoe . .
    irrigation and draining;
The currycomb . . the horse-cloth . . the halter and bridle
115   and bits . . the very wisps of straw,
The barn and barn-yard . . the bins and mangers . . the
    mows and racks:
Manufactures . . commerce . . engineering . . the building
    of cities, and every trade carried on there . . and the
    implements of every trade,
The anvil and tongs and hammer . . the axe and wedge . .
    the square and mitre and jointer and smoothingplane;
The plumbob and trowel and level . . the wall-scaffold, and
    the work of walls and ceilings . . or any mason-work:
The ship's compass . . the sailor's tarpaulin . . the stays
    and lanyards, and the ground-tackle for anchoring or
120   mooring,
The sloop's tiller . . the pilot's wheel and bell . . the yacht or
    fish-smack . . the great gay-pennanted three-hundred-
    foot steamboat under full headway, with her proud fat
    breasts and her delicate swift-flashing paddles;

The trail and line and hooks and sinkers . . the seine, and
    hauling the seine;
Smallarms and rifles . . . . the powder and shot and caps
    and wadding . . . . the ordnance for war . . . . the
    carriages:
Everyday objects . . . . the housechairs, the carpet, the bed
    and the counterpane of the bed, and him or her
    sleeping at night, and the wind blowing, and the
    indefinite noises:
The snowstorm or rainstorm . . . . the tow-trowsers . . . .
    the lodge-hut in the woods, and the still-hunt: 125
City and country . . fireplace and candle . . gaslight and
    heater and aqueduct;
The message of the governor, mayor, or chief of police . . . .
    the dishes of breakfast or dinner or supper;
The bunkroom, the fire-engine, the string-team, and the
    car or truck behind;
The paper I write on or you write on . . and every word
    we write . . and every cross and twirl of the pen . . and
    the curious way we write what we think . . . . yet very
    faintly;
The directory, the detector, the ledger . . . . the books in
    ranks or the bookshelves. . . . the clock attached to
    the wall,   130
The ring on your finger . . the lady's wristlet . . the
    hammers of stonebreakers or coppersmiths . . the
    druggist's vials and jars;
The etui of surgical instruments, and the etui of oculist's
    or aurist's instruments, or dentist's instruments;
Glassblowing, grinding of wheat and corn . . casting, and
    what is cast . . tinroofing, shingledressing,
Shipcarpentering, flagging of sidewalks by flaggers . .
    dockbuilding, fishcuring, ferrying;
The pump, the piledriver, the great derrick . . the coalkiln
    and brickkiln,   135
Ironworks or whiteleadworks . . the sugarhouse . . steam-
    saws, and the great mills and factories;

The cottonbale . . the stevedore's hook . . the saw and
    buck of the sawyer . . the screen of the coalscreener . .
    the mould of the moulder . . the workingknife of the
    butcher;
The cylinder press . . the handpress . . the frisket and
    tympan . . the compositor's stick and rule,
The implements for daguerreotyping . . . . the tools of the
    rigger or grappler or sailmaker or blockmaker,
Goods of guttapercha or papiermache . . . . colors and
140   brushes . . . . glaziers' implements,
The veneer and gluepot . . the confectioner's ornaments . .
    the decanter and glasses . . the shears and flatiron;
The awl and kneestrap . . the pint measure and quart
    measure . . the counter and stool . . the writingpen of
    quill or metal;
Billiards and tenpins . . . . the ladders and hanging ropes of
    the gymnasium, and the manly exercises;
The designs for wallpapers or oilcloths or carpets . . . . the
    fancies for goods for women . . . . the bookbinder's
    stamps;
Leatherdressing, coachmaking, boilermaking,
    ropetwisting, distilling, signpainting, limeburning,
145   coopering, cottonpicking,
The walkingbeam of the steam-engine . . the throttle and
    governors, and the up and down rods,
Stavemachines and planingmachines . . . . the cart of the
    carman . . the omnibus . . the ponderous dray;
The snowplough and two engines pushing it . . . . the ride
    in the express train of only one car . . . . the swift go
    through a howling storm:
The bearhunt or coonhunt . . . . the bonfire of shavings in
    the open lot in the city . . the crowd of children
    watching;
The blows of the fighting-man . . the upper cut and one-
150   two-three;
The shopwindows . . . . the coffins in the sexton's
    wareroom . . . . the fruit on the fruitstand . . . . the
    beef on the butcher's stall,

The bread and cakes in the bakery . . . . the white and red
    pork in the pork-store;
The milliner's ribbons . . the dressmaker's patterns . . . .
    the tea-table . . the homemade sweetmeats:
The column of wants in the one-cent paper . . the news
    by telegraph . . . . the amusements and operas and
    shows:
The cotton and woolen and linen you wear . . . . the money
    you make and spend;   155
Your room and bedroom . . . . your piano-forte . . . . the
    stove and cookpans,
The house you live in . . . . the rent . . . . the other
    tenants . . . . the deposit in the savings-bank . . . . the
    trade at the grocery,
The pay on Saturday night . . . . the going home, and the
    purchases;
In them the heft of the heaviest . . . . in them far more than
    you estimated, and far less also,
In them, not yourself . . . . you and your soul enclose all
    things, regardless of estimation,   160
In them your themes and hints and provokers . . if not,
    the whole earth has no themes or hints or provokers,
    and never had.

I do not affirm what you see beyond is futile . . . . I do not
    advise you to stop,
I do not say leadings you thought great are not great,
But I say that none lead to greater or sadder or happier
    than those lead to.

[6]
Will you seek afar off? You surely come back at last,
In things best known to you finding the best or as good as
    the best,   165
In folks nearest to you finding also the sweetest and
    strongest and lovingest,
Happiness not in another place, but this place . . not for
    another hour, but this hour,

Man in the first you see or touch . . . . always in your
    friend or brother or nighest neighbor . . . . Woman in
    your mother or lover or wife,
And all else thus far known giving place to men and
170   women.

When the psalm sings instead of the singer,
When the script preaches instead of the preacher,
When the pulpit descends and goes instead of the carver
    that carved the supporting desk,
When the sacred vessels or the bits of the eucharist, or the
    lath and plast, procreate as effectually as the young
    silversmiths or bakers, or the masons in their overalls,
When a university course convinces like a slumbering
175   woman and child convince,
When the minted gold in the vault smiles like the
    nightwatchman's daughter,
When warrantee deeds loafe in chairs opposite and are
    my friendly companions,
I intend to reach them my hand and make as much of
    them as I do of men and women.

LEAVES OF GRASS

[To Think of Time]

[1]

To think of time .... to think through the retrospection,
To think of today .. and the ages continued henceforward.
Have you guessed you yourself would not continue? Have
    you dreaded those earth-beetles?
Have you feared the future would be nothing to you?

Is today nothing? Is the beginningless past nothing?   5
If the future is nothing they are just as surely nothing.

To think that the sun rose in the east .... that men and
    women were flexible and real and alive .... that every
    thing was real and alive;
To think that you and I did not see feel think nor bear our
    part,
To think that we are now here and bear our part.

[2]

Not a day passes .. not a minute or second without an
    accouchement;   10
Not a day passes .. not a minute or second without a
    corpse.

When the dull nights are over, and the dull days also,
When the soreness of lying so much in bed is over,
When the physician, after long putting off, gives the silent
    and terrible look for an answer,

When the children come hurried and weeping, and the
15   brothers and sisters have been sent for,
When medicines stand unused on the shelf, and the
        camphor-smell has pervaded the rooms,
When the faithful hand of the living does not desert the
        hand of the dying,
When the twitching lips press lightly on the forehead of
        the dying,
When the breath ceases and the pulse of the heart ceases,
Then the corpse-limbs stretch on the bed, and the living
20   look upon them,
They are palpable as the living are palpable.

The living look upon the corpse with their eyesight,
But without eyesight lingers a different living and looks
        curiously on the corpse.

[3]
To think that the rivers will come to flow, and the snow
        fall, and fruits ripen . . and act upon others as upon
        us now . . . . yet not act upon us;
To think of all these wonders of city and country . . and
        others taking great interest in them . . and we taking
25   small interest in them.

To think how eager we are in building our houses,
To think others shall be just as eager . . and we quite
        indifferent.

I see one building the house that serves him a few
        years . . . . or seventy or eighty years at most;
I see one building the house that serves him longer than
        that.

Slowmoving and black lines creep over the whole earth . . . .
30   they never cease . . . . they are the burial lines,
He that was President was buried, and he that is now
        President shall surely be buried.

[4]
Cold dash of waves at the ferrywharf,
Posh and ice in the river . . . . half-frozen mud in the
    streets,
A gray discouraged sky overhead . . . . the short last
    daylight of December,
A hearse and stages . . . . other vehicles give place,   35
The funeral of an old stagedriver . . . . the cortege mostly
    drivers.

Rapid the trot to the cemetery,
Duly rattles the deathbell . . . . the gate is passed . . . . the
    grave is halted at . . . . the living alight . . . . the hearse
    uncloses,
The coffin is lowered and settled . . . . the whip is laid on
    the coffin,
The earth is swiftly shovelled in . . . . a minute . . no one
    moves or speaks . . . . it is done,   40
He is decently put away . . . . is there anything more?

He was a goodfellow,
Freemouthed, quicktempered, not badlooking, able to
    take his own part,
Witty, sensitive to a slight, ready with life or death for a
    friend,
Fond of women, . . played some . . eat hearty and drank
    hearty,   45
Had known what it was to be flush . . grew lowspirited
    toward the last . . sickened . . was helped by a
    contribution,
Died aged forty-one years . . and that was his funeral.

Thumb extended or finger uplifted,
Apron, cape, gloves, strap . . . . wetweather clothes . . . . whip
    carefully chosen . . . . boss, spotter, starter, and hostler,
Somebody loafing on you, or you loafing on
    somebody . . . . headway . . . . man before and man
    behind,   50

Good day's work or bad day's work . . . . pet stock or
    mean stock . . . . first out or last out . . . . turning in at
    night,
To think that these are so much and so nigh to other
    drivers . . . . and he there takes no interest in them.

[5]
The markets, the government, the workingman's
    wages . . . . to think what account they are through
    our nights and days;
To think that other workingmen will make just as great
    account of them . . yet we make little or no account.

The vulgar and the refined . . . . what you call sin and
    what you call goodness . . to think how wide a
55   difference;
To think the difference will still continue to others, yet
    we lie beyond the difference.

To think how much pleasure there is!
Have you pleasure from looking at the sky? Have you
    pleasure from poems?
Do you enjoy yourself in the city? or engaged in business?
    or planning a nomination and election? or with your
    wife and family?
Or with your mother and sisters? or in womanly
60   housework? or the beautiful maternal cares?

These also flow onward to others . . . . you and I flow
    onward;
But in due time you and I shall take less interest in them.

Your farm and profits and crops . . . . to think how
    engrossed you are;
To think there will still be farms and profits and crops . .
    yet for you of what avail?

[6]

What will be will be well—for what is is well,   65
To take interest is well, and not to take interest shall be well.

The sky continues beautiful . . . . the pleasure of men with
    women shall never be sated . . nor the pleasure of
    women with men . . nor the pleasure from poems;
The domestic joys, the daily housework or business, the
    building of houses—they are not phantasms . . they
    have weight and form and location;
The farms and profits and crops . . the markets and wages
    and government . . they also are not phantasms;   70
The difference between sin and goodness is no apparition;
The earth is not an echo . . . . man and his life and all the
    things of his life are well-considered.

You are not thrown to the winds . . you gather certainly
    and safely around yourself,
Yourself! Yourself! Yourself forever and ever!

[7]

It is not to diffuse you that you were born of your mother
    and father—it is to identify you,   75
It is not that you should be undecided, but that you should
    be decided;
Something long preparing and formless is arrived and
    formed in you,
You are thenceforth secure, whatever comes or goes.

The threads that were spun are gathered . . . . the weft
    crosses the warp . . . . the pattern is systematic.

The preparations have every one been justified;   80
The orchestra have tuned their instruments
    sufficiently . . . . the baton has given the signal.

The guest that was coming . . . . he waited long for
    reasons . . . . he is now housed,

He is one of those who are beautiful and happy . . . . he
    is one of those that to look upon and be with is
    enough.

The law of the past cannot be eluded,
85 The law of the present and future cannot be eluded,
The law of the living cannot be eluded . . . . it is eternal,
The law of promotion and transformation cannot be
    eluded,
The law of heroes and good-doers cannot be eluded,
The law of drunkards and informers and mean persons
    cannot be eluded.

[8]

Slowmoving and black lines go ceaselessly over the
90   earth,
Northerner goes carried and southerner goes carried . . . .
    and they on the Atlantic side and they on the Pacific,
    and they between, and all through the Mississippi
    country . . . . and all over the earth.
The great masters and kosmos are well as they go . . . . the
    heroes and good-doers are well,
The known leaders and inventors and the rich owners and
    pious and distinguished may be well,
But there is more account than that . . . . there is strict
    account of all.

The interminable hordes of the ignorant and wicked are
95   not nothing,
The barbarians of Africa and Asia are not nothing,
The common people of Europe are not nothing . . . . the
    American aborigines are not nothing,
A zambo or a foreheadless Crowfoot or a Camanche is
    not nothing,
The infected in the immigrant hospital are not
    nothing . . . . the murderer or mean person is not
    nothing,

The perpetual succession of shallow people are not
    nothing as they go, 100
The prostitute is not nothing . . . . the mocker of religion
    is not nothing as he goes.

I shall go with the rest . . . . we have satisfaction:
I have dreamed that we are not to be changed so
    much . . . . nor the law of us changed;
I have dreamed that heroes and good-doers shall be under
    the present and past law,
And that murderers and drunkards and liars shall be under
    the present and past law; 105
For I have dreamed that the law they are under now is
    enough.

And I have dreamed that the satisfaction is not so much
    changed . . . . and that there is no life without
    satisfaction;
What is the earth? what are body and soul without
    satisfaction?

I shall go with the rest,
We cannot be stopped at a given point . . . . that is no
    satisfaction; 110
To show us a good thing or a few good things for a space
    of time—that is no satisfaction;
We must have the indestructible breed of the best,
    regardless of time.

If otherwise, all these things came but to ashes of dung;
If maggots and rats ended us, then suspicion and treachery
    and death.

Do you suspect death? If I were to suspect death I should
    die now,
Do you think I could walk pleasantly and well-suited 115
    toward annihilation?

Pleasantly and well-suited I walk,
Whither I walk I cannot define, but I know it is good,
The whole universe indicates that it is good,
120 The past and the present indicate that it is good.

How beautiful and perfect are the animals! How perfect
    is my soul!
How perfect the earth, and the minutest thing upon it!
What is called good is perfect, and what is called sin is
    just as perfect;
The vegetables and minerals are all perfect . . and the
    imponderable fluids are perfect;
Slowly and surely they have passed on to this, and slowly
125   and surely they will yet pass on.

O my soul! if I realize you I have satisfaction,
Animals and vegetables! if I realize you I have
    satisfaction,
Laws of the earth and air! if I realize you I have
    satisfaction.

I cannot define my satisfaction . . yet it is so,
130 I cannot define my life . . yet it is so.

                        [9]
I swear I see now that every thing has an eternal soul!
The trees have, rooted in the ground . . . . the weeds of the
    sea have . . . . the animals.

I swear I think there is nothing but immortality!
That the exquisite scheme is for it, and the nebulous float
    is for it, and the cohering is for it,
And all preparation is for it . . and identity is for it . . and
135   life and death are for it.

LEAVES OF GRASS

[The Sleepers]

I wander all night in my vision,
Stepping with light feet . . . . swiftly and noiselessly
    stepping and stopping,
Bending with open eyes over the shut eyes of sleepers;
Wandering and confused . . . . lost to myself . . . . ill-
    assorted . . . . contradictory,
Pausing and gazing and bending and stopping.   5

How solemn they look there, stretched and still;
How quiet they breathe, the little children in their cradles.

The wretched features of ennuyees, the white features of
    corpses, the livid faces of drunkards, the sick-gray
    faces of onanists,
The gashed bodies on battlefields, the insane in their
    strong-doored rooms, the sacred idiots,
The newborn emerging from gates and the dying emerging
    from gates,   10
The night pervades them and enfolds them.

The married couple sleep calmly in their bed, he with his
    palm on the hip of the wife, and she with her palm on
    the hip of the husband,
The sisters sleep lovingly side by side in their bed,
The men sleep lovingly side by side in theirs,
And the mother sleeps with her little child carefully
    wrapped.   15

The blind sleep, and the deaf and dumb sleep,
The prisoner sleeps well in the prison . . . . the runaway
    son sleeps,
The murderer that is to be hung next day . . . . how does
    he sleep?
And the murdered person . . . . how does he sleep?

20   The female that loves unrequited sleeps,
And the male that loves unrequited sleeps;
The head of the moneymaker that plotted all day sleeps,
And the enraged and treacherous dispositions sleep.

I stand with drooping eyes by the worstsuffering and
    restless,
I pass my hands soothingly to and fro a few inches from
25   them;
The restless sink in their beds . . . . they fitfully sleep.

The earth recedes from me into the night,
I saw that it was beautiful . . . . and I see that what is not
    the earth is beautiful.

I go from bedside to bedside . . . . I sleep close with the
    other sleepers, each in turn;
30   I dream in my dream all the dreams of the other dreamers,
And I become the other dreamers.

I am a dance . . . . Play up there! the fit is whirling me fast.

I am the everlaughing . . . . it is new moon and twilight,
I see the hiding of douceurs . . . . I see nimble ghosts
    whichever way I look,
Cache and cache again deep in the ground and sea, and
35   where it is neither ground or sea.

Well do they do their jobs, those journeymen divine,
Only from me can they hide nothing and would not if
    they could;

I reckon I am their boss, and they make me a pet besides,
And surround me, and lead me and run ahead when I
     walk,
And lift their cunning covers and signify me with stretched
     arms, and resume the way;   40
Onward we move, a gay gang of blackguards with mirth-
     shouting music and wildflapping pennants of joy.

I am the actor and the actress . . . . the voter . . the politician,
The emigrant and the exile . . the criminal that stood in
     the box,
He who has been famous, and he who shall be famous
     after today,
The stammerer . . . . the wellformed person . . the wasted
     or feeble person.   45

I am she who adorned herself and folded her hair
     expectantly,
My truant lover has come and it is dark.

Double yourself and receive me darkness,
Receive me and my lover too . . . . he will not let me go
     without him.

I roll myself upon you as upon a bed . . . . I resign myself
     to the dusk.   50

He whom I call answers me and takes the place of my
     lover,
He rises with me silently from the bed.

Darkness you are gentler than my lover . . . . his flesh was
     sweaty and panting,
I feel the hot moisture yet that he left me.

My hands are spread forth . . I pass them in all directions,   55
I would sound up the shadowy shore to which you are
     journeying.

Be careful, darkness . . . . already, what was it touched
    me?
I thought my lover had gone . . . . else darkness and he are
    one,
I hear the heart-beat . . . . I follow . . I fade away.

60 O hotcheeked and blushing! O foolish hectic!
O for pity's sake, no one must see me now! . . . . my
    clothes were stolen while I was abed,
Now I am thrust forth, where shall I run?

Pier that I saw dimly last night when I looked from the
    windows,
Pier out from the main, let me catch myself with you and
    stay . . . . I will not chafe you;
65 I feel ashamed to go naked about the world,
And am curious to know where my feet stand . . . . and
    what is this flooding me, childhood or manhood . . . .
    and the hunger that crosses the bridge between.

The cloth laps a first sweet eating and drinking,
Laps life-swelling yolks . . . . laps ear of rose-corn, milky
    and just ripened:
The white teeth stay, and the boss-tooth advances in
    darkness,
And liquor is spilled on lips and bosoms by touching
70   glasses, and the best liquor afterward.

[2]
I descend my western course . . . . my sinews are flaccid,
Perfume and youth course through me, and I am their
    wake.

It is my face yellow and wrinkled instead of the old
    woman's,
I sit low in a strawbottom chair and carefully darn my
    grandson's stockings.

It is I too . . . . the sleepless widow looking out on the
    winter midnight,   75
I see the sparkles of starshine on the icy and pallid earth.

A shroud I see—and I am the shroud . . . . I wrap a body
    and lie in the coffin;
It is dark here underground . . . . it is not evil or pain
    here . . . . it is blank here, for reasons.

It seems to me that everything in the light and air ought to
    be happy;
Whoever is not in his coffin and the dark grave, let him
    know he has enough.   80

[3]

I see a beautiful gigantic swimmer swimming naked
    through the eddies of the sea,
His brown hair lies close and even to his head . . . . he
    strikes out with courageous arms . . . . he urges
    himself with his legs.

I see his white body . . . . I see his undaunted eyes;
I hate the swift-running eddies that would dash him
    headforemost on the rocks.

What are you doing you ruffianly red-trickled waves?   85
Will you kill the courageous giant? Will you kill him in
    the prime of his middle age?

Steady and long he struggles;
He is baffled and banged and bruised . . . . he holds out
    while his strength holds out,
The slapping eddies are spotted with his blood . . . . they
    bear him away . . . . they roll him and swing him and
    turn him:
His beautiful body is borne in the circling eddies . . . . it is
    continually bruised on rocks,   90
Swiftly and out of sight is borne the brave corpse.

[4]

I turn but do not extricate myself;
Confused . . . . a pastreading . . . . another, but with
        darkness yet.

The beach is cut by the razory ice-wind . . . . the wreck-
        guns sounds,
The tempest lulls and the moon comes floundering
95   through the drifts.

I look where the ship helplessly heads end on . . . . I hear
        the burst as she strikes . . I hear the howls of
        dismay . . . . they grow fainter and fainter.

I cannot aid with my wringing fingers;
I can but rush to the surf and let it drench me and freeze
        upon me.

I search with the crowd . . . . not one of the company is
        washed to us alive;
In the morning I help pick up the dead and lay them in
100   rows in a barn.

[5]

Now of the old war-days . . the defeat at Brooklyn;
Washington stands inside the lines . . he stands on the
        entrenched hills amid a crowd of officers,
His face is cold and damp . . . . he cannot repress the
        weeping drops . . . . he lifts the glass perpetually to
        his eyes . . . . the color is blanched from his
        cheeks,
He sees the slaughter of the southern braves confided to
        him by their parents.

105 The same at last and at last when peace is declared,
        He stands in the room of the old tavern . . . . the
        wellbeloved soldiers all pass through.

The officers speechless and slow draw near in their turns,
The chief encircles their necks with his arm and kisses
them on the cheek,
He kisses lightly the wet cheeks one after another . . . . he
shakes hands and bids goodbye to the army.

[6]
Now I tell what my mother told me today as we sat at
dinner together,   110
Of when she was a nearly grown girl living home with her
parents on the old homestead.

A red squaw came one breakfasttime to the old homestead,
On her back she carried a bundle of rushes for
rushbottoming chairs;
Her hair straight shiny coarse black and profuse
halfenveloped her face,
Her step was free and elastic . . . . her voice sounded
exquisitely as she spoke.   115

My mother looked in delight and amazement at the
stranger,
She looked at the beauty of her tallborne face and full and
pliant limbs,
The more she looked upon her she loved her,
Never before had she seen such wonderful beauty and
purity;
She made her sit on a bench by the jamb of the
fireplace . . . . she cooked food for her,   120
She had no work to give her but she gave her
remembrance and fondness.

The red squaw staid all the forenoon, and toward the
middle of the afternoon she went away;
O my mother was loth to have her go away,
All the week she thought of her . . . . she watched for her
many a month,

125   She remembered her many a winter and many a summer,
      But the red squaw never came nor was heard of there
           again.

      Now Lucifer was not dead . . . . or if he was I am his
           sorrowful terrible heir;
      I have been wronged . . . . I am oppressed . . . . I hate him
           that oppresses me,
      I will either destroy him, or he shall release me.

130   Damn him! how he does defile me,
      How he informs against my brother and sister and takes
           pay for their blood,
      How he laughs when I look down the bend after the
           steamboat that carries away my woman.

      Now the vast dusk bulk that is the whale's bulk . . . . it
           seems mine,
      Warily, sportsman! though I lie so sleepy and sluggish, my
           tap is death.

                              [7]
      A show of the summer softness . . . . a contact of
135   something unseen . . . . an amour of the light and air;
      I am jealous and overwhelmed with friendliness,
      And will go gallivant with the light and the air myself,
      And have an unseen something to be in contact with them
           also.

      O love and summer! you are in the dreams and in me,
      Autumn and winter are in the dreams . . . . the farmer
140   goes with his thrift,
      The droves and crops increase . . . . the barns are wellfilled.

      Elements merge in the night . . . . ships make tacks in the
           dreams . . . . the sailor sails . . . . the exile returns home,
      The fugitive returns unharmed . . . . the immigrant is
           back beyond months and years;

The poor Irishman lives in the simple house of his
    childhood, with the wellknown neighbors and faces,
They warmly welcome him . . . . he is barefoot again . . . .
    he forgets he is welloff;   145
The Dutchman voyages home, and the Scotchman and
    Welchman voyage home . . and the native of the
    Mediterranean voyages home;
To every port of England and France and Spain enter
    wellfilled ships;
The Swiss foots it toward his hills . . . . the Prussian goes
    his way, and the Hungarian his way, and the Pole goes
    his way,
The Swede returns, and the Dane and Norwegian return.

The homeward bound and the outward bound,   150
The beautiful lost swimmer, the ennuyee, the onanist, the
    female that loves unrequited, the moneymaker,
The actor and actress . . those through with their parts
    and those waiting to commence,
The affectionate boy, the husband and wife, the voter, the
    nominee that is chosen and the nominee that has
    failed,
The great already known, and the great anytime after to
    day,
The stammerer, the sick, the perfectformed, the homely,   155
The criminal that stood in the box, the judge that sat and
    sentenced him, the fluent lawyers, the jury, the
    audience,
The laugher and weeper, the dancer, the midnight widow,
    the red squaw,
The consumptive, the erysipalite, the idiot, he that is
    wronged,
The antipodes, and every one between this and them in
    the dark,
I swear they are averaged now . . . . one is no better than
    the other,   160
The night and sleep have likened them and restored
    them.

I swear they are all beautiful,
Every one that sleeps is beautiful . . . . every thing in the
    dim night is beautiful,
The wildest and bloodiest is over and all is peace.

165 Peace is always beautiful,
The myth of heaven indicates peace and night.

The myth of heaven indicates the soul;
The soul is always beautiful . . . . it appears more or it
    appears less . . . . it comes or lags behind,
It comes from its embowered garden and looks pleasantly
    on itself and encloses the world;
Perfect and clean the genitals previously jetting, and
170   perfect and clean the womb cohering,
The head wellgrown and proportioned and plumb, and
    the bowels and joints proportioned and plumb.

The soul is always beautiful,
The universe is duly in order . . . . every thing is in its place,
What is arrived is in its place, and what waits is in its
    place;
The twisted skull waits . . . . the watery or rotten blood
175   waits,
The child of the glutton or venerealee waits long, and the
    child of the drunkard waits long, and the drunkard
    himself waits long,
The sleepers that lived and died wait . . . . the far advanced
    are to go on in their turns, and the far behind are to
    go on in their turns,
The diverse shall be no less diverse, but they shall flow
    and unite . . . . they unite now.

[8]
The sleepers are very beautiful as they lie unclothed,
They flow hand in hand over the whole earth from east to
180   west as they lie unclothed;

The Asiatic and African are hand in hand . . the European
    and American are hand in hand,
Learned and unlearned are hand in hand . . and male and
    female are hand in hand;
The bare arm of the girl crosses the bare breast of her
    lover . . . . they press close without lust . . . . his lips
    press her neck,
The father holds his grown or ungrown son in his arms
    with measureless love . . . . and the son holds the
    father in his arms with measureless love,
The white hair of the mother shines on the white wrist of
    the daughter,   185
The breath of the boy goes with the breath of the
    man . . . . friend is inarmed by friend,
The scholar kisses the teacher and the teacher kisses the
    scholar . . . . the wronged is made right,
The call of the slave is one with the master's call . . and
    the master salutes the slave,
The felon steps forth from the prison . . . . the insane
    becomes sane . . . . the suffering of sick persons is
    relieved,
The sweatings and fevers stop . . the throat that was
    unsound is sound . . the lungs of the consumptive are
    resumed . . the poor distressed head is free,   190
The joints of the rheumatic move as smoothly as ever, and
    smoother than ever,
Stiflings and passages open . . . . the paralysed become
    supple,
The swelled and convulsed and congested awake to
    themselves in condition,
They pass the invigoration of the night and the chemistry
    of the night and awake.

I too pass from the night;   195
I stay awhile away O night, but I return to you again and
    love you;
Why should I be afraid to trust myself to you?

I am not afraid . . . . I have been well brought forward by
   you;
I love the rich running day, but I do not desert her in
   whom I lay so long:
I know not how I came of you, and I know not where I
   go with you . . . . but I know I came well and shall go
200   well.

I will stop only a time with the night . . . . and rise betimes.

I will duly pass the day O my mother and duly return to
   you;
Not you will yield forth the dawn again more surely than
   you will yield forth me again,
Not the womb yields the babe in its time more surely than
   I shall be yielded from you in my time.

LEAVES OF GRASS

[I Sing the Body Electric]

[1]

The bodies of men and women engirth me, and I engirth
  them,
They will not let me off nor I them till I go with them and
  respond to them and love them.

Was it dreamed whether those who corrupted their own
  live bodies could conceal themselves?
And whether those who defiled the living were as bad as
  they who defiled the dead?

[2]

The expression of the body of man or woman balks
  account,   5
The male is perfect and that of the female is perfect.

The expression of a wellmade man appears not only in his
  face,
It is in his limbs and joints also . . . . it is curiously in the
  joints of his hips and wrists,
It is in his walk . . the carriage of his neck . . the flex of
  his waist and knees . . . . dress does not hide him,
The strong sweet supple quality he has strikes through the
  cotton and flannel;   10
To see him pass conveys as much as the best poem . .
  perhaps more,
You linger to see his back and the back of his neck and
  shoulderside.

The sprawl and fulness of babes . . . . the bosoms and
    heads of women . . . . the folds of their dress . . . . their
    style as we pass in the street . . . . the contour of their
    shape downwards;
The swimmer naked in the swimmingbath . . seen as he
    swims through the salt transparent greenshine, or lies
    on his back and rolls silently with the heave of the
    water;
Framers bare-armed framing a house . . hoisting the
    beams in their places . . or using the mallet and
15   mortising-chisel,
The bending forward and backward of rowers in
    rowboats . . . . the horseman in his saddle;
Girls and mothers and housekeepers in all their exquisite
    offices,
The group of laborers seated at noontime with their open
    dinner-kettles, and their wives waiting,
The female soothing a child . . . . the farmer's daughter in
    the garden or cowyard,
The woodman rapidly swinging his axe in the woods . . . .
    the young fellow hoeing corn . . . . the sleighdriver
20   guiding his six horses through the crowd,
The wrestle of wrestlers . . . . two apprentice-boys, quite
    grown, lusty, goodnatured, nativeborn, out on the
    vacant lot at sundown after work,
The coats vests and caps thrown down . . the embrace of
    love and resistance,
The upperhold and underhold—the hair rumpled over and
    blinding the eyes;
The march of firemen in their own costumes—the play of
    the masculine muscle through cleansetting trowsers
    and waistbands,
The slow return from the fire . . . . the pause when the bell
25   strikes suddenly again—the listening on the alert,
The natural perfect and varied attitudes . . . . the bent
    head, the curved neck, the counting:
Suchlike I love . . . . I loosen myself and pass freely . . . .
    and am at the mother's breast with the little child,

And swim with the swimmer, and wrestle with wrestlers,
and march in line with the firemen, and pause and
listen and count.

[3]
I knew a man . . . . he was a common farmer . . . . he was the
father of five sons . . . . and in them were the fathers of
sons . . . . and in them were the fathers of sons.

This man was a wonderful vigor and calmness and beauty
of person;   30
The shape of his head, the richness and breadth of his
manners, the pale yellow and white of his hair and
beard, the immeasurable meaning of his black eyes,
These I used to go and visit him to see . . . . He was wise
also,
He was six feet tall . . . . he was over eighty years old . . . .
his sons were massive clean bearded tanfaced and
handsome,
They and his daughters loved him . . . all who saw him
loved him . . . they did not love him by allowance . . .
they loved him with personal love;
He drank water only . . . . the blood showed like scarlet
through the clear brown skin of his face;   35
He was a frequent gunner and fisher . . . he sailed his boat
himself . . . he had a fine one presented to him by a
shipjoiner . . . . he had fowling pieces, presented to
him by men that loved him;
When he went with his five sons and many grandsons to
hunt or fish you would pick him out as the most
beautiful and vigorous of the gang,
You would wish long and long to be with him . . . . you
would wish to sit by him in the boat that you and he
might touch each other.

[4]
I have perceived that to be with those I like is enough,
To stop in company with the rest at evening is enough,   40

To be surrounded by beautiful curious breathing laughing
    flesh is enough,
To pass among them . . to touch any one . . . . to rest my
    arm ever so lightly round his or her neck for a
    moment . . . . what is this then?
I do not ask any more delight . . . . I swim in it as in a sea.

There is something in staying close to men and women
    and looking on them and in the contact and odor of
    them that pleases the soul well,
45 All things please the soul, but these please the soul well.

[5]
This is the female form,
A divine nimbus exhales from it from head to foot,
It attracts with fierce undeniable attraction,
I am drawn by its breath as if I were no more than a
    helpless vapor . . . . all falls aside but myself and it,
Books, art, religion, time . . the visible and solid earth . . the
    atmosphere and the fringed clouds . . what was
50   expected of heaven or feared of hell are now consumed,
Mad filaments, ungovernable shoots play out of it . . the
    response likewise ungovernable,
Hair, bosom, hips, bend of legs, negligent falling hands—
    all diffused . . . . mine too diffused,
Ebb stung by the flow, and flow stung by the ebb . . . .
    loveflesh swelling and deliciously aching,
Limitless limpid jets of love hot and enormous . . . .
    quivering jelly of love . . . . white-blow and delirious
    juice,
Bridegroom-night of love working surely and softly into
55   the prostrate dawn,
Undulating into the willing and yielding day,
Lost in the cleave of the clasping and sweetfleshed day.

This is the nucleus . . . after the child is born of woman
    the man is born of woman,

This is the bath of birth . . . this is the merge of small and
    large and the outlet again.

Be not ashamed women . . your privilege encloses the
    rest . . it is the exit of the rest,   60
You are the gates of the body and you are the gates of the
    soul.

The female contains all qualities and tempers them . . . .
    she is in her place . . . . she moves with perfect
    balance,
She is all things duly veiled . . . . she is both passive and
    active . . . . she is to conceive daughters as well as sons
    and sons as well as daughters.

As I see my soul reflected in nature . . . . as I see through
    a mist one with inexpressible completeness and
    beauty . . . . see the bent head and arms folded over
    the breast . . . . the female I see,
I see the bearer of the great fruit which is immortality . . . .
    the good thereof is not tasted by roues, and never can
    be.   65

[6]
The male is not less the soul, nor more . . . . he too is in his
    place,
He too is all qualities . . . . he is action and power . . . . the
    flush of the known universe is in him,
Scorn becomes him well and appetite and defiance become
    him well,
The fiercest largest passions . . bliss that is utmost and
    sorrow that is utmost become him well . . . . pride is
    for him,
The fullspread pride of man is calming and excellent to
    the soul;   70
Knowledge becomes him . . . . he likes it always . . . . he
    brings everything to the test of himself,

Whatever the survey . . whatever the sea and the sail, he
    strikes soundings at last only here,
Where else does he strike soundings except here?

The man's body is sacred and the woman's body is
    sacred . . . . it is no matter who,
Is it a slave? Is it one of the dullfaced immigrants just
75   landed on the wharf?

Each belongs here or anywhere just as much as the
    welloff . . . . just as much as you,
Each has his or her place in the procession.

All is a procession,
The universe is a procession with measured and beautiful
    motion.

Do you know so much that you call the slave or the
80   dullfaced ignorant?
Do you suppose you have a right to a good sight . . . and
    he or she has no right to a sight?
Do you think matter has cohered together from its
    diffused float, and the soil is on the surface and water
    runs and vegetation sprouts for you . . and not for
    him and her?

[7]
A slave at auction!
I help the auctioneer . . . . the sloven does not half know
    his business.

85   Gentlemen look on this curious creature,
    Whatever the bids of the bidders they cannot be high
        enough for him,
    For him the globe lay preparing quintillions of years
        without one animal or plant,
    For him the revolving cycles truly and steadily rolled.

In that head the allbaffling brain,
In it and below it the making of the attributes of heroes.   90

Examine these limbs, red black or white . . . . they are very
    cunning in tendon and nerve;
They shall be stript that you may see them.

Exquisite senses, lifelit eyes, pluck, volition,
Flakes of breastmuscle, pliant backbone and neck, flesh
    not flabby, goodsized arms and legs,
And wonders within there yet.   95

Within there runs his blood . . . . the same old blood . . the
    same red running blood;
There swells and jets his heart . . . . There all passions and
    desires . . all reachings and aspirations:
Do you think they are not there because they are not
    expressed in parlors and lecture-rooms?

This is not only one man . . . . he is the father of those who
    shall be fathers in their turns,
In him the start of populous states and rich republics,   100
Of him countless immortal lives with countless
    embodiments and enjoyments.

How do you know who shall come from the offspring of
    his offspring through the centuries?
Who might you find you have come from yourself if you
    could trace back through the centuries?

                            [8]
A woman at auction,
She too is not only herself . . . . she is the teeming mother
    of mothers,   105
She is the bearer of them that shall grow and be mates to
    the mothers.

Her daughters or their daughters' daughters . . who knows
    who shall mate with them?

Who knows through the centuries what heroes may come
     from them?

In them and of them natal love . . . . in them the divine
     mystery . . . . the same old beautiful mystery.

110 Have you ever loved a woman?
     Your mother . . . . is she living? . . . . Have you been much
          with her? and has she been much with you?
     Do you not see that these are exactly the same to all in all
          nations and times all over the earth?

If life and the soul are sacred the human body is sacred;
And the glory and sweet of a man is the token of
     manhood untainted,
And in man or woman a clean strong firmfibred body is
115   beautiful as the most beautiful face.

Have you seen the fool that corrupted his own live body?
     or the fool that corrupted her own live body?
For they do not conceal themselves, and cannot conceal
     themselves.

Who degrades or defiles the living human body is cursed,
Who degrades or defiles the body of the dead is not more
     cursed.

LEAVES OF GRASS

[Faces]

[1]
Sauntering the pavement or riding the country byroads
    here then are faces,
Faces of friendship, precision, caution, sauvity, ideality,
The spiritual prescient face, the always welcome common
    benevolent face,
The face of the singing of music, the grand faces of
    natural lawyers and judges broad at the backtop,
The faces of hunters and fishers, bulged at the brows . . . .
    the shaved blanched faces of orthodox citizens,   5
The pure extravagant yearning questioning artist's face,
The welcome ugly face of some beautiful soul . . . . the
    handsome detested or despised face,
The sacred faces of infants . . . . the illuminated face of
    the mother of many children,
The face of an amour . . . . the face of veneration,
The face as of a dream . . . . the face of an immobile
    rock,   10
The face withdrawn of its good and bad . . a castrated
    face,
A wild hawk . . his wings clipped by the clipper,
A stallion that yielded at last to the thongs and knife of
    the gelder.

Sauntering the pavement or crossing the ceaseless ferry,
    here then are faces;
I see them and complain not and am content with all.   15

[2]
Do you suppose I could be content with all if I thought
    them their own finale?
This now is too lamentable a face for a man;
Some abject louse asking leave to be . . cringing for it,
Some milknosed maggot blessing what lets it wrig to its
    hole.

20 This face is a dog's snout sniffing for garbage;
Snakes nest in that mouth . . I hear the sibilant threat.

This face is a haze more chill than the arctic sea,
Its sleepy and wobbling icebergs crunch as they go.

This is a face of bitter herbs . . . . this an emetic . . . . they
    need no label,
And more of the drugshelf . . laudanum, caoutchouc, or
25   hog's lard.

This face is an epilepsy advertising and doing business . . . .
    its wordless tongue gives out the unearthly cry,
Its veins down the neck distend . . . . its eyes roll till they
    show nothing but their whites,
Its teeth grit . . the palms of the hands are cut by the
    turned-in nails,
The man falls struggling and foaming to the ground while
    he speculates well.

30 This face is bitten by vermin and worms,
And this is some murderer's knife with a halfpulled
    scabbard.

This face owes to the sexton his dismalest fee,
An unceasing deathbell tolls there.

Those are really men! . . . . the bosses and tufts of the
    great round globe!

[3]

Features of my equals, would you trick me with your
    creased and cadaverous march?   35
Well then you cannot trick me.

I see your rounded never-erased flow,
I see neath the rims of your haggard and mean disguises.

Splay and twist as you like . . . . poke with the tangling
    fores of fishes or rats,
You'll be unmuzzled . . . . you certainly will.   40

I saw the face of the most smeared and slobbering idiot
    they had at the asylum,
And I knew for my consolation what they knew not;
I knew of the agents that emptied and broke my brother,
The same wait to clear the rubbish from the fallen
    tenement;
And I shall look again in a score or two of ages,   45
And I shall meet the real landlord perfect and unharmed,
    every inch as good as myself.

[4]

The Lord advances and yet advances:
Always the shadow in front . . . . always the reached hand
    bringing up the laggards.

Out of this face emerge banners and horses . . . . O
    superb! . . . . I see what is coming,
I see the high pioneercaps . . . . I see the staves of runners
    clearing the way,   50
I hear victorious drums.

This face is a lifeboat;
This is the face commanding and bearded . . . . it asks no
    odds of the rest;
This face is flavored fruit ready for eating;

This face of a healthy honest boy is the programme of all
55   good.

These faces bear testimony slumbering or awake,
They show their descent from the Master himself.

Off the word I have spoken I except not one . . . . red
    white or black, all are deific,
In each house is the ovum . . . . it comes forth after a
    thousand years.

60 Spots or cracks at the windows do not disturb me,
Tall and sufficient stand behind and make signs to me;
I read the promise and patiently wait.

This is a fullgrown lily's face,
She speaks to the limber-hip'd man near the garden
    pickets,
Come here, she blushingly cries . . . . Come nigh to me
65   limber-hip'd man and give me your finger and thumb,
Stand at my side till I lean as high as I can upon you,
Fill me with albescent honey . . . . bend down to me,
Rub to me with your chafing beard . . rub to my breast
    and shoulders.

[5]
The old face of the mother of many children:
70 Whist! I am fully content.

Lulled and late is the smoke of the Sabbath morning,
It hangs low over the rows of trees by the fences,
It hangs thin by the sassafras, the wildcherry and the
    catbrier under them.

I saw the rich ladies in full dress at the soiree,
75 I heard what the run of poets were saying so long,
Heard who sprang in crimson youth from the white froth
    and the water-blue.

Behold a woman!
She looks out from her quaker cap . . . . her face is clearer
    and more beautiful than the sky.

She sits in an armchair under the shaded porch of the
    farmhouse,
The sun just shines on her old white head.   80

Her ample gown is of creamhued linen,
Her grandsons raised the flax, and her granddaughters
    spun it with the distaff and the wheel.

The melodious character of the earth!
The finish beyond which philosophy cannot go and does
    not wish to go!
The justified mother of men!   85

[Song of the Answerer]

A young man came to me with a message from his
    brother,
How should the young man know the whether and when
    of his brother?
Tell him to send me the signs.

And I stood before the young man face to face, and took
    his right hand in my left hand and his left hand in my
    right hand,
And I answered for his brother and for men . . . . and I
5   answered for the poet, and sent these signs.

Him all wait for . . . . him all yield up to . . . . his word is
    decisive and final,
Him they accept . . . . in him lave . . . . in him perceive
    themselves as amid light,
Him they immerse, and he immerses them.

Beautiful women, the haughtiest nations, laws, the
    landscape, people and animals,
The profound earth and its attributes, and the unquiet
10   ocean,
All enjoyments and properties, and money, and whatever
    money will buy,
The best farms . . . . others toiling and planting, and he
    unavoidably reaps,
The noblest and costliest cities . . . . others grading and
    building, and he domiciles there;

Nothing for any one but what is for him . . . . near and far
    are for him,
The ships in the offing . . . . the perpetual shows and
    marches on land are for him if they are for any body.   15

He puts things in their attitudes,
He puts today out of himself with plasticity and love,
He places his own city, times, reminiscences, parents,
    brothers and sisters, associations employment and
    politics, so that the rest never shame them afterward,
    nor assume to command them.

He is the answerer,
What can be answered he answers, and what cannot be
    answered he shows how it cannot be answered.   20

A man is a summons and challenge,
It is vain to skulk . . . . Do you hear that mocking and
    laughter? Do you hear the ironical echoes?

Books friendships philosophers priests action pleasure
    pride beat up and down seeking to give satisfaction;
He indicates the satisfaction, and indicates them that beat
    up and down also.

Whichever the sex . . . whatever the season or place he
    may go freshly and gently and safely by day or by
    night,   25
He has the passkey of hearts . . . . to him the response of
    the prying of hands on the knobs.

His welcome is universal . . . . the flow of beauty is not
    more welcome or universal than he is,
The person he favors by day or sleeps with at night is
    blessed.

Every existence has its idiom . . . . every thing has an idiom
    and tongue;

He resolves all tongues into his own, and bestows it upon
    men . . and any man translates . . and any man
30   translates himself also:
One part does not counteract another part . . . . He is the
    joiner . . he sees how they join.

He says indifferently and alike, How are you friend? to
    the President at his levee,
And he says Good day my brother, to Cudge that hoes in
    the sugarfield;
And both understand him and know that his speech is
    right.

35   He walks with perfect ease in the capitol,
He walks among the Congress . . . . and one representative
    says to another, Here is our equal appearing and new.

Then the mechanics take him for a mechanic,
And the soldiers suppose him to be a captain . . . . and the
    sailors that he has followed the sea,
And the authors take him for an author . . . . and the
    artists for an artist,
And the laborers perceive he could labor with them and
40   love them;
No matter what the work is, that he is one to follow it or
    has followed it,
No matter what the nation, that he might find his brothers
    and sisters there.

The English believe he comes of their English stock,
A Jew to the Jew he seems . . . . a Russ to the Russ . . . .
    usual and near . . removed from none.

Whoever he looks at in the traveler's coffeehouse claims
45   him,
The Italian or Frenchman is sure, and the German is sure,
    and the Spaniard is sure . . . . and the island Cuban is
    sure.

The engineer, the deckhand on the great lakes or on the
    Mississippi or St. Lawrence or Sacramento or Hudson
    or Delaware claims him.

The gentleman of perfect blood acknowledges his perfect
    blood,
The insulter, the prostitute, the angry person, the beggar,
    see themselves in the ways of him . . . . he strangely
    transmutes them,
They are not vile any more . . . . they hardly know
    themselves, they are so grown.   50

You think it would be good to be the writer of melodious
    verses,
Well it would be good to be the writer of melodious
    verses;
But what are verses beyond the flowing character you
    could have? . . . . or beyond beautiful manners and
    behaviour?
Or beyond one manly or affectionate deed of an
    apprenticeboy? . . . . or old woman? . . or man that
    has been in prison or is likely to be in prison?

[Europe: The 72d and 73d Years of These States]

Suddenly out of its stale and drowsy lair, the lair of slaves,
Like lightning Europe le'pt forth . . . . half startled at itself,
Its feet upon the ashes and the rags . . . . Its hands tight to
the throats of kings.

O hope and faith! O aching close of lives! O many a
sickened heart!
5 Turn back unto this day, and make yourselves afresh.

And you, paid to defile the People . . . . you liars mark:
Not for numberless agonies, murders, lusts,
For court thieving in its manifold mean forms,
Worming from his simplicity the poor man's wages;
For many a promise sworn by royal lips, and broken, and
10 laughed at in the breaking,
Then in their power not for all these did the blows strike
of personal revenge . . or the heads of the nobles fall;
The People scorned the ferocity of kings.

But the sweetness of mercy brewed bitter destruction, and
the frightened rulers come back:
Each comes in state with his train . . . . hangman, priest
and tax-gatherer . . . . soldier, lawyer, jailer and
sycophant.

15 Yet behind all, lo, a Shape,
Vague as the night, draped interminably, head front and
form in scarlet folds,

Whose face and eyes none may see,
Out of its robes only this . . . . the red robes, lifted by the
    arm,
One finger pointed high over the top, like the head of a
    snake appears.
Meanwhile corpses lie in new-made graves . . . . bloody
    corpses of young men: 20
The rope of the gibbet hangs heavily . . . . the bullets of
    princes are flying . . . . the creatures of power laugh
    aloud,
And all these things bear fruits . . . . and they are good.

Those corpses of young men,
Those martyrs that hang from the gibbets . . . those hearts
    pierced by the gray lead,
Cold and motionless as they seem . . live elsewhere with
    unslaughter'd vitality. 25

They live in other young men, O kings,
They live in brothers, again ready to defy you:
They were purified by death . . . . they were taught and
    exalted.

Not a grave of the murdered for freedom but grows seed
    for freedom . . . . in its turn to bear seed,
Which the winds carry afar and re-sow, and the rains and
    the snows nourish. 30

Not a disembodied spirit can the weapons of tyrants let
    loose,
But it stalks invisibly over the earth . . whispering
    counseling cautioning.

Liberty let others despair of you . . . . I never despair of you.

Is the house shut? Is the master away?
Nevertheless be ready . . . . be not weary of watching, 35
He will soon return . . . . his messengers come anon.

[A Boston Ballad]

Clear the way there Jonathan!
Way for the President's marshal! Way for the government
    cannon!
Way for the federal foot and dragoons . . . . and the
    phantoms afterward.

I rose this morning early to get betimes in Boston town;
Here's a good place at the corner . . . . I must stand and
5   see the show.

I love to look on the stars and stripes . . . . I hope the fifes
    will play Yankee Doodle.

How bright shine the foremost with cutlasses,
Every man holds his revolver . . . . marching stiff through
    Boston town.

A fog follows . . . . antiques of the same come limping,
Some appear wooden-legged and some appear bandaged
10   and bloodless.

Why this is a show! It has called the dead out of the earth,
The old graveyards of the hills have hurried to see;
Uncountable phantoms gather by flank and rear of it,
Cocked hats of mothy mould and crutches made of mist,
Arms in slings and old men leaning on young men's
15   shoulders.

What troubles you, Yankee phantoms? What is all this
    chattering of bare gums?
Does the ague convulse your limbs? Do you mistake your
    crutches for firelocks, and level them?
If you blind your eyes with tears you will not see the
    President's marshal,
If you groan such groans you might balk the government
    cannon.

For shame old maniacs! . . . . Bring down those tossed
    arms, and let your white hair be;   20
Here gape your smart grandsons . . . . their wives gaze at
    them from the windows,
See how well-dressed . . . . see how orderly they conduct
    themselves.

Worse and worse . . . . Can't you stand it? Are you
    retreating?
Is this hour with the living too dead for you?

Retreat then! Pell-mell! . . . . Back to the hills, old limpers!   25
I do not think you belong here anyhow.

But there is one thing that belongs here . . . . Shall I tell
    you what it is, gentlemen of Boston?

I will whisper it to the Mayor . . . . he shall send a
    committee to England,
They shall get a grant from the Parliament, and go with a
    cart to the royal vault.
Dig out King George's coffin . . . . unwrap him quick
    from the graveclothes . . . . box up his bones for a
    journey: 30
Find a swift Yankee clipper . . . . here is freight for you
    blackbellied clipper,
Up with your anchor! shake out your sails! . . . . steer
    straight toward Boston bay.

Now call the President's marshal again, and bring out the
    government cannon,
And fetch home the roarers from Congress, and make
    another procession and guard it with foot and
    dragoons.

35 Here is a centrepiece for them:
Look! all orderly citizens . . . . look from the windows
    women.

The committee open the box and set up the regal ribs and
    glue those that will not stay,
And clap the skull on top of the ribs, and clap a crown on
    top of the skull.

You have got your revenge old buster! . . . . The crown is
    come to its own and more than its own.

Stick your hands in your pockets Jonathan . . . . you are a
40   made man from this day,
You are mighty cute . . . . and here is one of your bargains.

[There Was a Child Went Forth]

There was a child went forth every day,
And the first object he looked upon and received with
    wonder or pity or love or dread, that object he
    became,
And that object became part of him for the day or a
    certain part of the day . . . . or for many years or
    stretching cycles of years.

The early lilacs became part of this child,
And grass, and white and red morningglories, and white
    and red clover, and the song of the phœbe-bird,   5
And the March-born lambs, and the sow's pink-faint
    litter, and the mare's foal, and the cow's calf, and the
    noisy brood of the barnyard or by the mire of the
    pondside . . and the fish suspending themselves so
    curiously below there . . and the beautiful curious
    liquid . . and the water-plants with their graceful flat
    heads . . all became part of him.

And the field-sprouts of April and May became part of
    him . . . . wintergrain sprouts, and those of the light-
    yellow corn, and of the esculent roots of the garden,
And the appletrees covered with blossoms, and the fruit
    afterward . . . . and woodberries . . and the commonest
    weeds by the road;
And the old drunkard staggering home from the outhouse
    of the tavern whence he had lately risen,

And the schoolmistress that passed on her way to the
school . . and the friendly boys that passed . . and the
quarrelsome boys . . and the tidy and freshcheeked
10   girls . . and the barefoot negro boy and girl,
And all the changes of city and country wherever he
went.

His own parents . . he that had propelled the fatherstuff at
night, and fathered him . . and she that conceived him
in her womb and birthed him . . . . they gave this child
more of themselves than that,
They gave him afterward every day . . . . they and of them
became part of him.

The mother at home quietly placing the dishes on the
suppertable,
The mother with mild words . . . . clean her cap and
gown . . . . a wholesome odor falling off her person
15   and clothes as she walks by:
The father, strong, selfsufficient, manly, mean, angered,
unjust,
The blow, the quick loud word, the tight bargain, the
crafty lure,
The family usages, the language, the company, the
furniture . . . . the yearning and swelling heart,
Affection that will not be gainsayed . . . . The sense of
what is real . . . . the thought if after all it should
prove unreal,
The doubts of daytime and the doubts of nighttime . . . the
20   curious whether and how,
Whether that which appears so is so . . . . Or is it all
flashes and specks?
Men and women crowding fast in the streets . . if they are
not flashes and specks what are they?
The streets themselves, and the facades of houses . . . . the
goods in the windows,
Vehicles . . teams . . the tiered wharves, and the huge
crossing at the ferries;

The village on the highland seen from afar at sunset . . . .
    the river between,   25
Shadows . . aureola and mist . . light falling on roofs and
    gables of white or brown, three miles off,
The schooner near by sleepily dropping down the tide . .
    the little boat slacktowed astern,
The hurrying tumbling waves and quickbroken crests and
    slapping;
The strata of colored clouds . . . . the long bar of
    maroontint away solitary by itself . . . . the spread of
    purity it lies motionless in,
The horizon's edge, the flying seacrow, the fragrance of
    saltmarsh and shoremud;   30
These became part of that child who went forth every day,
    and who now goes and will always go forth every day,
And these become of him or her that peruses them now.

[Who Learns My Lesson Complete?]

Who learns my lesson complete?
Boss and journeyman and apprentice? . . . . churchman
and atheist?
The stupid and the wise thinker . . . . parents and
offspring . . . . merchant and clerk and porter and
customer . . . . editor, author, artist and schoolboy?

Draw nigh and commence,
5   It is no lesson . . . . it lets down the bars to a good lesson,
And that to another . . . . and every one to another still.

The great laws take and effuse without argument,
I am of the same style, for I am their friend,
I love them quits and quits . . . . I do not halt and make
salaams.

I lie abstracted and hear beautiful tales of things and the
10   reasons of things,
They are so beautiful I nudge myself to listen.

I cannot say to any person what I hear . . . . I cannot say it
to myself . . . . it is very wonderful.

It is no little matter, this round and delicious globe,
moving so exactly in its orbit forever and ever,
without one jolt or the untruth of a single second;
I do not think it was made in six days, nor in ten thousand
years, nor ten decillions of years,

Nor planned and built one thing after another, as an
    architect plans and builds a house. 15

I do not think seventy years is the time of a man or woman,
Nor that seventy millions of years is the time of a man or
    woman,
Nor that years will ever stop the existence of me or any
    one else.
Is it wonderful that I should be immortal? as every one is
    immortal,
I know it is wonderful . . . . but my eyesight is equally
    wonderful . . . . and how I was conceived in my
    mother's womb is equally wonderful, 20
And how I was not palpable once but am now . . . . and
    was born on the last day of May 1819 . . . . and passed
    from a babe in the creeping trance of three summers
    and three winters to articulate and walk . . . . are all
    equally wonderful.

And that I grew six feet high . . . . and that I have become
    a man thirty-six years old in 1855 . . . . and that I am
    here anyhow—are all equally wonderful;
And that my soul embraces you this hour, and we affect
    each other without ever seeing each other, and never
    perhaps to see each other, is every bit as wonderful:
And that I can think such thoughts as these is just as
    wonderful,
And that I can remind you, and you think them and know
    them to be true is just as wonderful, 25
And that the moon spins round the earth and on with the
    earth is equally wonderful,
And that they balance themselves with the sun and stars is
    equally wonderful.

Come I should like to hear you tell me what there is in
    yourself that is not just as wonderful,
And I should like to hear the name of anything between
    Sunday morning and Saturday night that is not just as
    wonderful.

[Great Are the Myths]

Great are the myths . . . . I too delight in them,
Great are Adam and Eve . . . . I too look back and accept
  them;
Great the risen and fallen nations, and their poets,
  women, sages, inventors, rulers, warriors and
  priests.

Great is liberty! Great is equality! I am their follower,
Helmsmen of nations, choose your craft . . . . where you
5   sail I sail,
Yours is the muscle of life or death . . . . yours is the perfect
  science . . . . in you I have absolute faith.

Great is today, and beautiful,
It is good to live in this age . . . . there never was any
  better.

Great are the plunges and throes and triumphs and falls
  of democracy,
10 Great the reformers with their lapses and screams,
Great the daring and venture of sailors on new
  explorations.

Great are yourself and myself,
We are just as good and bad as the oldest and youngest
  or any,
What the best and worst did we could do,

What they felt . . do not we feel it in ourselves?   15
What they wished . . do we not wish the same?

Great is youth, and equally great is old age . . . . great are
    the day and night;
Great is wealth and great is poverty . . . . great is
    expression and great is silence.

Youth large lusty and loving . . . . youth full of grace and
    force and fascination,
Do you know that old age may come after you with equal
    grace and force and fascination?   20

Day fullblown and splendid . . . . day of the immense sun,
    and action and ambition and laughter,
The night follows close, with millions of suns, and sleep
    and restoring darkness.

Wealth with the flush hand and fine clothes and
    hospitality:
But then the soul's wealth—which is candor and
    knowledge and pride and enfolding love:
Who goes for men and women showing poverty richer
    than wealth?   25

Expression of speech . . in what is written or said forget
    not that silence is also expressive,
That anguish as hot as the hottest and contempt as cold as
    the coldest may be without words,
That the true adoration is likewise without words and
    without kneeling.

[2]
Great is the greatest nation . . the nation of clusters of
    equal nations.

Great is the earth, and the way it became what it is,   30
Do you imagine it is stopped at this? . . . . and the increase
    abandoned?

Understand then that it goes as far onward from this as
  this is from the times when it lay in covering waters
  and gases.

Great is the quality of truth in man,
The quality of truth in man supports itself through all
  changes,
It is inevitably in the man . . . . He and it are in love, and
35   never leave each other.

The truth in man is no dictum . . . . it is vital as eyesight,
If there be any soul there is truth . . . . if there be man or
  woman there is truth . . . . If there be physical or
  moral there is truth,
If there be equilibrium or volition there is truth . . . . if
  there be things at all upon the earth there is truth.

O truth of the earth! O truth of things! I am determined
  to press the whole way toward you,
Sound your voice! I scale mountains or dive in the sea
40   after you.

[3]
Great is language . . . . it is the mightiest of the sciences,
It is the fulness and color and form and diversity of the
  earth . . . . and of men and women . . . . and of all
  qualities and processes;
It is greater than wealth . . . . it is greater than buildings or
  ships or religions or paintings or music.

Great is the English speech . . . . What speech is so great as
  the English?
Great is the English brood . . . . What brood has so vast a
45   destiny as the English?
It is the mother of the brood that must rule the earth with
  the new rule,
The new rule shall rule as the soul rules, and as the love
  and justice and equality that are in the soul rule.

Great is the law . . . . Great are the old few landmarks of
the law . . . . they are the same in all times and shall
not be disturbed.
Great are marriage, commerce, newspapers, books,
freetrade, railroads, steamers, international mails and
telegraphs and exchanges.

[4]

Great is Justice;   50
Justice is not settled by legislators and laws . . . . it is in the
soul,
It cannot be varied by statutes any more than love or pride
or the attraction of gravity can,
It is immutable . . it does not depend on majorities . . . .
majorities or what not come at last before the same
passionless and exact tribunal.

For justice are the grand natural lawyers and perfect
judges . . . . it is in their souls,
It is well assorted . . . . they have not studied for
nothing . . . . the great includes the less,   55
They rule on the highest grounds . . . . they oversee all eras
and states and administrations,

The perfect judge fears nothing . . . . he could go front to
front before God,
Before the perfect judge all shall stand back . . . . life and
death shall stand back . . . . heaven and hell shall stand
back.

[5]

Great is goodness;
I do not know what it is any more than I know what
health is . . . . but I know it is great.   60

Great is wickedness . . . . I find I often admire it just as
much as I admire goodness:
Do you call that a paradox? It certainly is a paradox.

The eternal equilibrium of things is great, and the eternal
    overthrow of things is great,
And there is another paradox.

Great is life . . and real and mystical . . wherever and
    whoever,
Great is death . . . . Sure as life holds all parts together,
    death holds all parts together;
Sure as the stars return again after they merge in the light,
    death is great as life.

The Portable Walt Whitman
Edited by Michael Warner
When Walt Whitman self-published *Leaves of Grass* in 1855, it was a slim volume of twelve poems, alarmingly unfamiliar in form, shockingly frank, unabashedly American, and aggressively democratic. At the time, Whitman was a journalist from Long Island, unknown but full of ambition; at his death in 1892, he was beginning to be recognized as one of the most distinctive poetic voices of the modern world. He had spent his entire lifetime revising and adding to his work, which broke new ground in its treatment of the individual, eroticism, mortality, and the trauma of the Civil War. This rich cross section includes poems from throughout Whitman's lifetime, the early short story "The Child's Champion," his prefaces to the many editions of *Leaves of Grass*, and a variety of prose selections, including *Democratic Vistas, Specimen Days,* and "Slang in America."   *ISBN 0-14-243768-9*

The Complete Poems
Edited with an Introductory Note by Francis Murphy
This volume features Whitman's final "death-bed" edition (1891–1892) of *Leaves of Grass*—the work that defined him as one of America's most influential voices—as well ass earlier versions of many of the poems, given in the notes, so that the reader can follow the poet's development. Apart from manuscript fragments, this edition contains all of Whitman's known poetic work.   *ISBN 0-14-042451-2*

Nineteenth-Century American Poetry
Edited with an Introduction and Notes by
William C. Spengemann with Jessica F. Roberts
Whitman, Dickinson, and Melville occupy the center of this anthology of nearly three hundred poems, spanning the course of the century, from Joel Barlow to Edwin Arlington Robinson.
ISBN 0-14-043587-5

T. S. Eliot
The Waste Land and Other Poems
Edited with an Introduction and Notes by Frank Kermode
This new edition collects all of the poems published in Eliot's first three volumes of verse, including "The Love Song of J. Alfred Prufrock," "Portrait of a Lady," "Gerontion," "Sweeny Among the Nightingales," and "Whispers of Immortality."
ISBN 0-14-243731-X

Robert Frost
Early Poems: A Boy's Will, North of Boston,
Mountain Interval, and Other Poems
Edited with an Introduction and Notes by Robert Faggen
This volume presents Frost's first three books, masterful and innovative collections that contain some of his best-known poems, including "Mowing," "Mending Wall," "After Apple-Picking," "Home Burial," "The Oven Bird," and "The Road Not Taken."
ISBN 0-14-118017-X

James Weldon Johnson
Complete Poems
Edited with an Introduction by Sondra Kathryn Wilson
This volume brings together all of Johnson's published works, a number of previously unpublished poems, and reflections on his pioneering contributions to recording and celebrating the African American experience.
ISBN 0-14-118545-7

Henry Wadsworth Longfellow
Selected Poems
Edited with an Introduction and Notes by Lawrence Buell
Longfellow was the most popular poet of his day. This selection
includes generous samplings from his longer works—*Evangeline,
The Courtship of Miles Standish*, and *Hiawatha*—as well as his
shorter lyrics and less familiar narrative poems.
ISBN 0-14-039064-2

Edna St. Vincent Millay
Early Poems
Edited with an Introduction and Notes by Holly Peppe
Millay's first three books of lyrics and sonnets are collected here:
Renascence, Second April, and *A Few Figs from Thistles*. With a
balanced introduction and useful annotations, this volume pres-
ents some of the Pulitzer Prize–winning poet's best work.
ISBN 0-14-118054-4

Ezra Pound
Early Writings
Edited with an Introduction and Notes by Ira Nadel
This unique selection of Pound's early work includes such mas-
terpieces of poetry as "The Seafarer" and the first eight of
Pound's incomparable "Cantos," with prose selections of more
than thirty essays, articles, and critical pieces, including the
famous "Chinese Written Character as a Medium for Poetry."
ISBN 0-14-218013-0

Edwin Arlington Robinson
Selected Poems
Edited with an Introduction by Robert Faggen
Finely crafted, formal rhythms mirror the tension the poet sees
between life's immutable circumstances and humanity's often
tragic attempts to exert control. At once dramatic and witty,
these poems lay bare the tyranny of love and unspoken, unno-
ticed suffering.
ISBN 0-14-018988-2

The Last of the Mohicans
James Fenimore Cooper
Introduction by Richard Slotkin
Tragic, fast-paced, and stocked with the elements of a classic Western adventure, this novel takes Natty Bumppo and his Indian friend Chingachgook through hostile Indian territory during the French and Indian War. *ISBN 0-14-039024-3*

Two Years Before the Mast: A Personal Narrative of Life at Sea
Richard Henry Dana, Jr.
Edited with an Introduction and Notes by Thomas Philbrick
Dana's account of his passage as a common seaman from Boston around Cape Horn to California and back is a remarkable portrait that forever changed readers' romanticized perceptions of life at sea.
ISBN 0-14-039008-1

Nature and Selected Essays
Ralph Waldo Emerson
Edited with an Introduction by Larzer Ziff
This sampling includes fifteen essays that highlight the formative and significant ideas of this central American thinker.
ISBN 0-14-243762-X

The Scarlet Letter
Nathaniel Hawthorne
Introduction by Nina Baym with Notes by Thomas E. Connolly
Hawthorne's novel of guilt and redemption in pre-Revolutionary Massachusetts provides vivid insight into the social and religious forces that shaped early America. *ISBN 0-14-243726-3*

The Legend of Sleepy Hollow and Other Stories
Washington Irving
Introduction and Notes by William L. Hedges
Irving's delightful 1819 miscellany of essays and sketches includes the two classic tales "The Legend of Sleepy Hollow" and "Rip Van Winkle." *ISBN 0-14-043769-X*

The Portable Abraham Lincoln
Abraham Lincoln
Edited by Andrew Delbanco
The essential Lincoln, including all of the great public speeches, along with less familiar letters and memoranda that chart Lincoln's political career. With an indispensable introduction, headnotes, and a chronology of Lincoln's life. *ISBN 0-14-017031-6*

The Fall of the House of Usher and Other Writings
Edgar Allan Poe
Edited with an Introduction and Notes by David Galloway
This selection includes seventeen poems, among them "The Raven,"
"Annabel Lee," and "The Bells"; nineteen tales, including "The Fall of
the House of Usher," "The Murders in the Rue Morgue," "The Tell-
Tale Heart," "The Masque of the Red Death," and "The Pit and the
Pendulum"; and sixteen essays and reviews.   *ISBN 0-14-143981-5*

Uncle Tom's Cabin
Or, Life Among the Lowly
Harriet Beecher Stowe
Edited with an Introduction by Ann Douglas
Perhaps the most powerful document in the history of American abo-
litionism, this controversial novel goaded thousands of readers to
take a stand on the issue of slavery and played a major political and
social role in the Civil War period.   *ISBN 0-14-039003-0*

Walden and Civil Disobedience
Henry David Thoreau
Introduction by Michael Meyer
Two classic examinations of individuality in relation to nature, socie-
ty, and government. "Civil Disobedience" is perhaps the most famous
essay in American literature—and the inspiration for social activists
around the world, from Gandhi to Martin Luther King, Jr.
ISBN 0-14-039044-8

The Education of Henry Adams
Henry Adams
Edited with an Introduction and Notes by Jean Gooder
A remarkable synthesis of history, art, politics, and philosophy. In this
memoir Adams examines his own life as it reflects the progress of the
United States from the Civil War period to the nation's ascendancy as
a world power.   *ISBN 0-14-044557-9*

Little Women
Louisa May Alcott
Edited with an Introduction by Elaine Showalter
Notes by Siobhan Kilfeather and Vinca Showalter
Alcott's beloved story of the March girls—Meg, Jo, Beth, and Amy—
is a classic American feminist novel, reflecting the tension between
cultural obligation and artistic and personal freedom.
ISBN 0-14-039069-3

Looking Backward: 2000–1887
Edward Bellamy
Edited with an Introduction by Cecelia Tichi
When first published in 1888, *Looking Backward* initiated a national political- and social-reform movement. This profoundly utopian tale addresses the anguish and hope of its age, as well as having lasting value as an American cultural landmark.   *ISBN 0-14-039018-9*

Tales of Soldiers and Civilians and Other Stories
Ambrose Bierce
Edited with an Introduction and Notes by Tom Quirk
This collection gathers three dozen of Bierce's finest tales of war and the supernatural, including "An Occurrence at Owl Creek Bridge" and "The Damned Thing."   *ISBN 0-14-043756-8*

The Awakening and Selected Stories
Kate Chopin
Edited with an Introduction by Sandra M. Gilbert
First published in 1899, *The Awakening* recounts the transformation of Edna Pontellier, who claims for herself moral and erotic freedom. Other selections include "Emancipation," "At the 'Cadian Ball," and "Désirée's Baby."   *ISBN 0-14-243709-3*

The Red Badge of Courage and Other Stories
Stephen Crane
Edited with an Introduction by Pascal Covici, Jr.
One of the greatest novels ever written about war and its psychological effects on the individual soldier. This edition also includes the short stories "The Open Boat," "The Bride Comes to Yellow Sky," "The Blue Hotel," "A Poker Game," and "The Veteran."
    ISBN 0-14-039081-2

Personal Memoirs
Ulysses S. Grant
Introduction and Notes by James M. McPherson
Grant's memoirs demonstrate the intelligence, intense determination, and laconic modesty that made him the Union's foremost commander.
    ISBN 0-14-043701-0

The Luck of Roaring Camp and Other Writings
Bret Harte
Edited with an Introduction by Gary Scharnhorst
More than any other writer, Harte was at the forefront of western
American literature. This volume brings together all of his best-
known pieces, as well as a selection of his poetry, lesser-known essays,
and three of his hilarious condensed novels—parodies of James
Fenimore Cooper, Charles Dickens, and Sir Arthur Conan Doyle.
ISBN 0-14-043917-X

A Hazard of New Fortunes
William Dean Howells
Introduction by Phillip Lopate
Set against a vividly depicted background of fin de siècle New York,
A Hazard of New Fortunes is both a memorable portrait of an era
and a profoundly moving study of human relationships.
ISBN 0-14-043923-4

The Portrait of a Lady
Henry James
Edited with an Introduction by Geoffrey Moore
and Notes by Patricia Crick
Regarded by many critics as James's masterpiece, this is the story of
Isabel Archer, an independent American heiress captivated by the lan-
guid charms of an Englishman.   ISBN 0-14-143963-7

The Country of the Pointed Firs and Other Stories
Sarah Orne Jewett
Edited with an Introduction by Alison Easton
In this richly detailed portrait of a seaport on the Maine coast as seen
through the eyes of summer visitors, Jewett interweaves conversations
and stories, capturing the spirit of community that sustains the declin-
ing town.   ISBN 0-14-043476-3